DIY PICKLING

A PECK OF PICKLED PEPPERS

Is the craft of pickling new to you? Get started with these simple do-it-yourself pickling projects and unleash the kitchen crafter in you.

- **A CLASSIC REFRIGERATED DILL PICKLE** (page 30) is the perfect place to start. Find troubleshooting tips and illustrations to guide you.

- **SAUERKRAUT** (page 58) will be your fermentation primer. Use this basic recipe to learn techniques you will turn to again and again.

- **CURIOUS ABOUT PICKLED FRUIT?** Prepare this recipe for Pickled Pears (page 84) and you'll be a fruit pickle convert.

- **START EXPERIMENTING WITH TSUKEMONO** like Takuan (page 109), a classic Japanese pickle that is work the wait.

Happy pickling!

DIY PICKLING

STEP-BY-STEP RECIPES FOR FERMENTED, FRESH, AND QUICK PICKLES

ROCKRIDGE PRESS

For general information on our other products and services or to obtain technical support, please contact our Customer Care Department within the United States at (866) 744-2665, or outside the United States at (510) 253-0500.

Rockridge Press publishes its books in a variety of electronic and print formats. Some content that appears in print may not be available in electronic books, and vice versa.

TRADEMARKS: Rockridge Press and the Rockridge Press logo are trademarks or registered trademarks of Callisto Media Inc. and/or its affiliates, in the United States and other countries, and may not be used without written permission. All other trademarks are the property of their respective owners. Rockridge Press is not associated with any product or vendor mentioned in this book.

Front cover photography © Offset/Lucy Schaeffer; Back cover photography © Stockfood/Kathryn Russell; Interior photography © Stockfood/Kathryn Russell, p.2 & 144; Stockfood/Tate Carlson, p.2 & 26; Stockfood/Oliver Brachat, p.3; Stocksy/Renáta Dobránska, p.6; Getty/Westend61, p.9; Stocksy/Jill Chen, p.10; Stockfood/Rua Castilho, p.18; Stockfood/Eising Studio - Food Photo & Video, p.33; Stockfood/Victoria Firmston, p.34; Stockfood/és-cuisine, p.56; Stockfood/People Pictures, p.80; Stockfood/Rua Castilho, p.98; Stockfood/Eising Studio - Food Photo & Video, p.122; Stockfood/Chugrad McAndrews, p.156

Illustrations © 2015 by Tom Bingham

ISBN: Print 978-1-62315-663-3 | eBook 978-1-62315-687-9

CONTENTS

INTRODUCTION

Do you love the crisp bite of a fresh pickle? Or how about the pungent, yet addictive flavor of kimchi or sauerkraut? Whether you prefer spicy, sweet, or something in between, this ultimate do-it-yourself pickling book has got you covered. Now you can turn everyday garden produce into a medley of pickled products with these simple, time-tested methods of food preservation.

Every day millions of people enjoy the taste of pickled food unique to their own region of the world. In many countries, eating pickled foods is just part of the daily routine. In Korea, kimchi is king, served in countless variations. In Japan, just about every meal is paired with some form of tsukemono, a unique variety of both fresh and fermented pickles that span a wide taste zone. Eastern Europeans round out meals with pickled turnips and beets, and sauerkraut is widely served throughout this region and into Germany, where it is highlighted in the signature sausage and sauerkraut dish. In short, these pickled food items are so much a part of

> The recent focus on the health benefits of fermented food and the surge in home pickling has introduced a multitude of pickled delicacies from around the globe, and made this a fun and delicious craft.

everyday eating that they've become a large part of the ethnic food of the region, and are beloved on tables across the globe.

In America, the pickling lexicon has largely been limited to staples such as dill pickles, relish, and ketchup, but there is so much more to explore. The recent focus on the health benefits of fermented food and the surge in home pickling have introduced a multitude of pickled delicacies from around the globe, and made this a fun and delicious craft.

If you are looking for a way to incorporate more local food in your diet, pickling is a great way to start. Not only does it provide you with a variety of quick, convenient foods in your refrigerator or pantry, it can also help save you money. Buying local food in season is the best way to trim excess costs from your grocery bill while still eating healthily. When foods are readily available, they are at their cheapest, so this is the most cost-effective time to head to the market to gather your ingredients for pickling.

Combining a variety of styles, this DIY guide and recipe collection contains plenty to offer the beginner as well as those with several pickling projects already under their belts. Featuring easy-to-follow recipes for both fresh and fermented pickling projects, this book breaks down the pickling process so you are assured success. Put the "home" back in *homemade* with this assortment of diverse recipes. Immerse yourself in the tradition of cooks and picklers from around the globe, and enliven your taste buds on the journey. Enjoy the process and happy pickling!

PICKLING 101

I

1

YOUR PICKLING PRIMER

The roots of pickling lie in the age-old practice of food preservation. Created as a way to stretch the harvest, these simple processes can dramatically extend the shelf life of food in a way that is otherwise not possible. Before refrigeration, most fresh produce wouldn't survive a week in the heat of the summer months. But through the near-magical capabilities of pickling, foods can be eaten for weeks, and in the case of canned pickles, up to a year after the harvest.

FROM THE MASTERS

ROB SEUFERT, OWNER/PICKLER OF EPIC PICKLES, YORK, PA

www.epicpickles.com

When did I start pickling? This is probably the question I get asked the most. It began with an article about a "pickle guy" and an artisan movement in food. So with a few bucks and some research, a business was born. And those neighbors knocking on my door looking for pickles didn't hurt either.

I've never gotten much advice in my adventure, but I say this to everyone who asks about pickling or who wants to help—"it's not rocket science!" While there's definitely a science to it, it's more an art—a craft. And it's easy to overthink the process, but under think the preparation. First, the process. Brine, veggies, seasonings—done. Start simple and go from there. And mistakes are the best teachers—just make sure you learn from them! Second, the preparation. If you've never heard, it's exactly true that you first eat with your eyes, then your mouth. Make sure your pickles look as good as they taste. One without the other and your ship will sink. Good luck!

Epic Pickles was born in 2011 from a passion for fabulous food. In this case, pickles! Founder Rob Seufert tried his first "flavored" pickle and the rest is history. Small batches, hand crafted, fresh ingredients, fabulous flavor—in a word, it's "Epic"!

Pickling foods in vinegar dates back to 1,000 BCE in the Middle East, where plums, pears, and apples were preserved with spices, and in the third century BCE, the Chinese experimented with fermentation to provide laborers working on the Great Wall of China with fermented vegetables as part of their daily food rations.

Throughout the centuries in Asia, a variety of pickling methods were developed depending on the regional climate and available produce. In Japan, for instance, salted vegetables, fermented bran pickles, and other fermented pickles were widely prepared throughout the country. The Japanese also use vinegar, soy sauce, and miso to create the starkly contrasted quick pickles. Korean pickles are typically fermented and several types of vinegared pickles are common, such as pickled garlic in vinegar.

The Romans brought the art of pickling with vinegar to Western Europe, and centuries later, Western and Eastern European immigrants brought it to the United States. Vinegar had been the predominant method used in pickling in the early 1900s, but then sugar became widely available in the United States and fruits were pickled as chutneys, ketchups, and other relishes. By the time home canning came into play shortly before World War II, pickling foods had become a common practice in many kitchens around America, but its popularity waned in subsequent decades as processed foods moved to the forefront.

Pickling has seen a resurgence in recent years, with many artisanal pickling producers popping up around the country to support the growing trend. Today, you can draw on all these different styles of pickling to create something special for your family, as families have done around the world for centuries. There are no boundaries to the pickles you can explore. With produce and seeds so widely available today for growing whatever produce you desire, there is no reason not to try your hand at this age-old craft, and in doing so, expand your palate.

THE BENEFITS OF PICKLING

Whether your main concern is improving your health or stretching your pocketbook, there are several reasons why pickling at home can be a good option for you.

EXTEND SHELF LIFE

Pickling foods extends their shelf life. Naturally, decomposition would begin in just days at room temperature, but through fermentation, many items can be stored for weeks. And when pickled foods are canned, the shelf life typically extends to one year. By pickling foods, you can take a large harvest from your garden (or bought in bulk at the farmers' market) and prepare a variety of items that will last beyond the growing season.

PROVIDE PROBIOTICS

Pickling foods traditionally through fermentation is a great way to get a healthy dose of probiotics on a daily basis. Probiotics, important for providing your digestive tract with healthy bacteria that improve digestion and promote overall health, are considered beneficial for all people. When you make traditionally pickled products through fermentation, you are growing these healthy bacteria and yeasts yourself that will then colonize your digestive tract and help your body fight infection, improve immunity, and minimize digestive distress. In addition, since fermented foods have already begun the process of breaking down, they are easier for your body to digest than the same foods served raw.

INCREASE FLAVOR

Pickling foods increases their flavor and allows you to add hints of additional flavors. For example, cucumbers can taste bland on their own, but when infused with dill, garlic, and other spices, their flavor comes alive and really shines. This is true with so many types of produce, and makes pickling a great way to try new foods that may never have seemed appealing before. If you don't like the sourness of pickles, keep in mind that there are also several types of sweet pickles, as well as some varieties that are not as pronouncedly sour as others. It is this wide range of flavors that make pickles so appealing to so many people.

INCREASE FRUIT AND VEGETABLE INTAKE

Fermented pickles are arguably a better option regarding advantages for your health, but even quick pickling provides health benefits. If pickling enables you to eat more fruits and vegetables regularly, it can be a convenient way to increase your consumption and, consequently, increase the amount of valuable vitamins and minerals you are putting in your body. While quick-pickled foods don't have the probiotic benefits of fermented foods, pickled carrots, beets, asparagus, and other vegetables contain a wealth of nutrients your body needs, and add more veggies to your diet in a delicious and unique way.

SAVE MONEY

Pickling foods yourself lets you eat a wide variety of gourmet-quality foods at half the price. When produce is at the height of its season, it is at its lowest prices, so this is the best time to snag some deals and get started on a pickling project. You can have pickled vegetables all year long, beyond the growing season, and because you do all of the labor yourself in making the end product, you pay no additional cost—not the case with the myriad artisanal pickled products lining the shelves of supermarkets.

ALL THE PICKLES

The term *pickle* is best known as the soured cucumber you get in a delicatessen or jarred on the supermarket shelf, but pickle refers to any soured food made through different processes, which can take anywhere from minutes to weeks to complete.

There are several different types of pickling that we'll explore in this book. While the end result may taste similar in its mouth-puckeringly sour crunch, some distinctly different practices can create very diverse results.

FRESH PICKLES

Fresh pickles are the quick-pickling choice and are the most common type of pickles found in supermarkets. Soured using a mixture of an acetic acid (most commonly vinegar) and water, they are typically flavored with salt, a variety of spices, and sometimes sugar. Most canned pickle recipes are this type of quick-process pickles. These pickles can span the gamut of pickled food items, from vegetables to fruits to even eggs.

The term *fresh* in this pickle's title means they have not been fermented, but soured just enough to retain their bright color, crispy texture, and fresh taste. Despite being called "fresh" they are not ready to eat when the recipe is complete, but rather, many fresh pickles must be stored from days to weeks to obtain their full flavor.

FERMENTED PICKLES

Fermentation is the process of using bacteria and yeast to convert the sugar in foods to acid or alcohol. In pickling, this process is called *lacto-fermentation*. Bacteria and yeast produce lactic acid, giving pickles their desired sour flavor. In order to prevent spoilage, salt or a starter culture is added. Starter cultures can include

FAQ: WHAT'S THE DIFFERENCE BETWEEN PICKLING AND FERMENTATION?

Pickling is a broad term that describes all foods that have been purposely soured. Many people think the two words—*pickling* and *fermentation*—are interchangeable, but they are not. Quick pickling uses vinegar or another acidic medium, while lacto-fermentation, the type of fermentation used to make pickles, requires a starter culture or salt. The end result produced by both taste similar, but the process to arrive there is completely different.

All food items made sour by adding an acid can be considered pickled. Quick, fresh pickles using vinegar, lemon juice, or citrus can include many foods. The end result is, for instance, cucumber pickles, pickled beans, pickled asparagus, pickled strawberries, chutneys, and relishes.

Foods such as old-fashioned dill pickles, sauerkraut, and kimchi are typically made through the addition of salt and left to sit for a longer time until lactic acid causes the bubbling action signaling fermentation. In these cases, the foods are both pickled and fermented. (Wine is also fermented but because grapes are high in sugar, it turns into alcohol rather than lactic acid.)

Most pickled products made through quick pickling can also be made using fermentation; therefore, to determine if a commercial food is made through fermentation or fresh pickling, check the label. When food is produced through fermentation, the label will most likely tell you so, but the main clue is an ingredient list that includes only items such as vegetables, salt, and spices, and does not include vinegar or another acidic substance.

whey, kombucha, or commercially prepared starter cultures.

Fermented pickles can be just as sour as fresh pickles, but the actual processing time is much longer. Fermented foods, such as fruits, can take just a day or two, but harder foods like carrots and beets and those containing less sugar can require several weeks to obtain full sourness. While this process may sound complex, it is actually quite manageable and safe in the home kitchen where it originated and has taken place for hundreds of years.

CHUTNEYS

Chutneys are a type of pickled condiment that uses a wide variety of fruits, spices, and vegetables. Most common in South Asian cuisine, these fruity, tangy mixtures can range considerably in their consistency, ingredients, and heat level. Typically divided into sweet and hot varieties, chutneys are preserved using vinegar, lemon juice, or citrus, as well as through fermentation. Fruit is most commonly the base for chutney, though vegetables can make an appearance as well. Common seasonings are garlic, onion, ginger, coriander, cumin, cilantro, and mint. Chutneys are often paired with meats, poultry, and fish, or can be served with breads and other grain-based dishes.

RELISHES

Relishes, like chutneys, are largely condiments as well. Originating in India like chutneys, the term *relish* today most commonly applies to Western staples such as sweet pickle relish,

zucchini relish, and corn relish. Relishes are also closely related to ketchups and salsas, and are very similar to chutneys in their complexity, but are often associated with more Western-style flavors. Relishes can be made with whole, ground, or infused spices, and in the case of ketchup and other similar condiments, can be puréed into a thick sauce. Other types of relish can be used on sandwiches, in dips, and as spreads.

PICKLING METHODS

There are a few different methods for pickling various types of foods. While pickling is a rather simple method of food preservation, the process will vary slightly based on what foods you are pickling. The following are the three main types of pickling used in this book.

SALT

Pickling using salt is primarily a method used for fermentation. Salt is used to process foods such as cabbage that once salted have enough natural moisture to produce a brine. By drawing the water from the vegetable, salt pickling leaves the pickled vegetables crisp, yet changed from their original state. Salt protects food during fermentation from bacteria and yeasts that would otherwise cause decomposition to take place. This allows for the good bacteria and yeasts, also present in the air we breathe, to take hold and transform the sugars in the food to lactic acid. Once this transformation is complete, the lactic acid protects the pickled food from spoilage. Japanese pickling also employs salt pickling, although in this case, the pickling process is typically stopped before fermentation takes place. Salt is also added to quick-process pickles, but in this case it is for flavor and not preservation.

BRINE

Using a brine is another method of fermentation pickling. For this method, you create a mixture of salt, water, and spices, then submerge the produce into this brine until the pickling is complete. Depending on the food item, this can take a matter of days or several weeks. A brine is used for foods that would not otherwise create their own liquid through dry salting, such as carrots, cucumbers, beets, and beans. This method is also used for making kimchi. The term *brine* additionally applies to a liquid mixture made with vinegar and used for fresh pickling.

VINEGAR

Vinegar is used for quick, fresh pickling. Any type of vinegar, as long as it is 5 percent acidity, is fair game for pickling, though different recipes call for different types, based on the desired flavor of the finished pickles. Apple cider vinegar, distilled white vinegar, and white wine vinegar are all commonly used to obtain that pickled flavor. When pickles are made through vinegar pickling, vinegar is typically mixed with water, salt, and spices to create a tangy brine. It is sometimes added to fermented pickles, as well, at the end of fermentation to extend shelf life.

FAQ: IS PICKLING DANGEROUS?

Pickling is a traditional craft that has been practiced for generations. While you should maintain basic food sanitation measures in your kitchen, there is no need to worry about pickling being dangerous. Be sure to thoroughly clean all items used for pickling in warm, soapy water before you begin, and carefully follow directions to ensure success.

If you are canning your pickles, you need to follow a recipe specifically designed for canning to prevent spoilage or bacteria leaking into the jar. Not all types of pickles can be canned, and it is important that if you want to can pickles you follow a recipe for doing so. Additionally, you should make sure you are up-to-date with the most current canning practices and familiar with how to operate your water-bath canner (see FAQ: Do I Need to Can My Pickles? page 23).

With both fermented and fresh pickles, there is the chance that something may go wrong, such as mold growth, off flavors, or other spoilage. However, by simply inspecting your pickled foods before eating, you should easily be able to determine if this is the case. If there is a problem, you will know it. Smell, texture, and visible observation will give you the clues you need to determine the safety of a pickled food. As with any food item, if it seems off, do not taste it to check. Instead, discard the food safely in a place inaccessible to humans and animals, and then clean and sanitize the storage container and workspace thoroughly.

2
THE PICKLER'S KITCHEN

Be wary of the rabbit hole of endless kitchen tools when you begin pickling. In fact, there are just a few basics you'll need to get started in this craft. While there certainly is no lack of fancy fermenting, canning, and pickling equipment available, there is no need to go overboard buying supplies for your kitchen. Gather the following essential ingredients and equipment, and you'll be pickling in no time—without all the fuss.

ESSENTIAL INGREDIENTS

As you explore the recipes in this book, you may come across some lesser-known ingredients, but many of the necessary items can typically be found in your kitchen already. Start with these basics to begin the pickling process. As you progress, you may want to invest in more, but it's best to start simple and work your way up to more complex recipes as your confidence grows.

SALT

Salt is important in both quick pickles and fermented pickles. First and foremost, it provides flavor. However, you don't want to just reach for your table salt, as it contains additives that are used to prevent caking, but in pickling, create a cloudy mess. Instead, choose a salt that has no added filler. Pickling and canning salt is a simple choice and can be found at most well-stocked grocery stores. Sea salt can also be used if it is pure, though be sure to avoid any colored sea salt. Because the term *sea salt* is not regulated, make sure to check the label for any additives before using it for pickling. Kosher salt can also be used, but because it has larger crystals, it will have to be heated with the brine to dissolve completely in the water. Additionally, to account for the larger crystal size, you will need to substitute about one and a half times as much kosher salt for other fine salts.

VINEGARS

There are many types of vinegar available for use in pickling. In the United States, all commercial vinegars are formulated between 4 and 6 percent acetic acid, with most at 5 percent. Homemade vinegars can be quite variable and should not be used unless you can verify their acetic acid level by testing their pH. It is recommended that you always use commercial vinegars for pickling, particularly when canning your pickles. If you are canning your pickles, you should always use 5 percent acetic acid vinegar—you'll find this information listed on the label. Distilled white vinegar, apple cider vinegar, wine vinegar, rice vinegar, and malt vinegar are all viable options for pickling. It is also essential that you do not reduce the quantity of vinegar in a recipe, as this can potentially make the pickle unsafe to eat. In general, fresh pickles should be made using one part vinegar to one part water. Do not boil the water and vinegar for an extended period, as this can decrease the acetic acid in the brine, since acetic acid evaporates at a faster rate than water. Always be sure to follow recipe recommendations on boiling time.

WATER

You may or may not be able to use your tap water for pickling purposes. If it tastes good and doesn't contain a significant amount of chlorine or other minerals, it can most likely be used. If it's not usable, opt for distilled or filtered water.

If your water stains your sink with iron deposits, you must remedy this before using the water for pickling, or these deposits will end up in your jars. To treat the water, boil the water in a pot, and then leave it to sit for 24 hours. Skim the water from the top, leaving any sediment behind. For chlorinated water, boil the water for 2 minutes to eliminate the chlorine, or let it sit overnight before using.

AROMATICS

Dill is synonymous with pickling and widely used, especially when it comes to cucumbers. In the summer, fresh dill is available, but if you are pickling out of season, dill seeds work well too. Other popular aromatics used in pickling include garlic, ginger, juniper berries, cloves, mace, cumin, and coriander. Whole, crushed, and ground spices can all be utilized in the pickling process. Whole spices make a nice appearance in a jar, while ground spices add lots of flavor quickly, but can leave many pickles looking murky. Follow recipe directions for the type of pickle you are making. In some cases, a spice bag is the best option for infusing the strong flavor of whole spices into a pickled item. A scrap of cheesecloth provides a simple solution for making a spice bag.

EQUIPMENT OVERVIEW

You don't need a bunch of fancy equipment to get started pickling. Sure, you could spend a lot of money on specialized pickling implements, but it is in no way necessary. Starting small and scaling up if you decide that you love the art of pickling is a sensible way to go.

KITCHEN TOOLS

KITCHEN SCALE: For the most precision, a kitchen scale is recommended to ensure that accurate quantities of produce and ingredients are used. Because volume and number equivalents do not always match, this is the best way to ensure your results. You can always measure produce at the market if you do not have a kitchen scale, but it is much more convenient to have one at home. They are reasonably priced (under $20) and make a great addition to your kitchen.

BOWLS AND POTS: Because pickling widely uses both salt and vinegar, which are both quite reactive, it is important that you use nonreactive cookware and bowls when making pickled products from this book. On the range, both stainless steel and hard-anodized aluminum pots and pans work well, while stainless steel, glass, and ceramic are all good options for bowls.

UTENSILS: A nonreactive spoon and ladle are needed for many of the recipes in this book. Stainless steel, wood, or plastic utensils make the best choices.

FERMENTATION VESSEL: You will also need a vessel in which to ferment your pickles. This can either be glass or ceramic. Large quart and 2-quart mason jars are good fermentation vessels, and in some cases, a bowl can be used as well. For smaller batches, there are a few different types of jars available, which are fitted with an airlock to help with the anaerobic process. These are easy to use and are often sold with weights to help keep fermenting foods submerged below the brine.

WEIGHTS: The fermentation recipes in this book require that the produce is weighted during fermentation to prevent the food being exposed to oxygen. For this purpose, a ceramic plate, small jar, or clean rock can be used. If you use

Pickling equipment (clockwise from top left): Jar lifter, Assorted mason jars with lids, Funnels (small and large), Jar with airlock, Digital kitchen scale, Pot with canning rack, Mixing bowls (small and large).

wide-mouth canning jars, a regular-mouth jelly jar fits nicely in the mouth of the jar as a weight. In smaller jars, a votive candle holder or a food-safe, plastic-zippered bag filled with brine can also be used to hold the produce below the brine. Whichever you choose, the same principles for nonreactive items, such as the bowls and pots, apply here as well.

CANNING SUPPLIES: If you plan on canning your pickles, at the very least you will need a small canning setup. A large, deep pot with a lid will suffice for a water-bath canner. A drying rack, towel, or canning rack will also be needed to keep the jars off the surface of the pot to prevent breakage. Other necessary tools are a jar filler, a jar lifter, and two-piece canning lids.

FAQ: DO I NEED TO CAN MY PICKLES?

The recipes in this book are all designed for small-batch pickling and do not need to be canned. In fact, many kinds of pickles are made to be eaten within several days of pickling and should never be canned because the salt content in the pickles is too low to prevent spoilage.

In some cases, however, pickles can be canned. When this is possible, a note is made in the recipe to indicate this. But unless the recipe indicates canning, *do not can the pickles*.

When you do can pickles, the water-bath canning method can be used. This simple preservation method is highly accessible for all, and by following a few simple steps, you too can prepare your own pickles for the darker months of the year. Review the following steps before beginning any water-bath canning project.

- **ASSEMBLE THE EQUIPMENT:** You will need a large pot for water-bath canning that allows the jars you are using to be submerged by at least 1 inch. You will also need a rack that fits into the pot to keep the jars off the bottom of the pot and prevent breakage. An old cake rack works, as does a folded kitchen towel in a pinch. There are also racks that fit a smaller pot available where home-canning supplies are sold. You will also need canning jars and two-piece lids for canning. Everything should be washed in warm, soapy water and air dried before use.

- **PREPARE THE CANNER:** Fill the canner halfway with water and add the rack to the pot. Heat the water. For cold-packed foods, heat the water to about 140°F, and for hot-packed foods, heat the water to 180°F. The cooler temperature of the water for cold-packed foods helps prevent breakage when the jars are immersed in the water. Once submerged, the temperature will be brought to boiling in either case.

- **PREPARE THE JARS, LIDS, AND RINGS:** Wash the jars, lids, and rings in hot, soapy water. If your recipe requires you to process the jars for more than 10 minutes, set the jars aside until you are ready to pack them. If your recipe requires less than 10 minutes of processing, add the jars to the canner and bring the water to a boil for 10 minutes to sterilize them. Once the time is complete, remove the jars from the water, keep the tops off, and bring the temperature back down to the appropriate level based on whether you are doing a cold pack or hot pack. Set the lids and rings aside to dry.

- **PREPARE YOUR RECIPE:** While the water is heating (or jars sterilizing), prepare your recipe.

- **FILL THE JARS:** Pack the recipe into jars, using a ladle and jar funnel to get the ingredients in easily and mess-free. Fill the jars with the brine to the appropriate level indicated in the recipe. Remove air bubbles from the jar using a nonreactive utensil inserted into the jar and moved around the jar's inner surface. If needed, adjust the contents of the jar to the correct level after removing the air bubbles.

- **AFFIX THE LIDS:** Wipe the rims of the jars clean using a clean, damp kitchen towel. Place the lid, centered, on the jar and affix it with the ring. Turn the ring until it is tight to the touch using your thumb, index, and middle fingers. Do not over-tighten the ring or leave it too loose.

- **PROCESS THE JARS:** Using a jar lifter, place the filled jars into the canner. Ensure that the water is covering the tops of the jars by at least 1 inch. If it is not, add more hot water now. Place the lid on the pot and turn the heat up. Once a rolling boil occurs, start the timer and process the jars according to the time indicated in the recipe. If you live at 1,000 feet above sea level or higher, you will need to adjust your processing time accordingly. See the Appendix (page 159) to do this. When the timer goes off, turn off the heat, remove the lid, and allow the jars to cool in the water for 5 minutes. Using a jar lifter, carefully remove the jars and place them on a cutting board or kitchen towel on the counter.

- **STORE THE JARS:** After the jars cool, check for a seal. The center of the lid should be concave, and you should be able to lift the jar by its top. If the seal did not work, place the jar in the refrigerator. Otherwise, remove the rings (to prevent rust), and store the jars in a cool, dark place for up to 1 year.

STORAGE

JARS: Mason jars in several different sizes are typically all that is needed to store your pickles. If you are canning your pickles, you want to stock up on these in half-pint, pint, and quart sizes. For refrigerator storage, you can also use half-gallon jars. If you are not planning on canning pickles, old repurposed glass jars are a fine alternative to mason jars. However, these should never be used for canning, as they are designed for single use and are not as sturdy as mason jars, nor do they have the correct lid.

LIDS: For pickle storage, it is a good idea to invest in plastic lids that fit onto mason jars. These are available in wide-mouth and narrow-mouth sizes from any retailer that sells canning supplies. These prevent a reaction caused by the acidic nature of pickles in contact with a reactive metal. While canning lids in theory will not react with pickles, if the lid is nicked or damaged, a reaction takes place that will cause the lid to rust. For this reason, you should line a canning lid with a couple of layers of plastic wrap if you are going to use one for storing pickles.

TROUBLESHOOTING TIPS

As you begin pickling, you will undoubtedly have some questions about the process, and even wonder if something you made is safe to eat. Starting out, it may be difficult to tell whether a new pickle is as it should be, or perhaps just not something you are used to eating, especially when making pickled items that are foreign to your taste buds.

Pickling introduces some new smells to the kitchen that you may not find familiar. That doesn't necessarily mean that they are bad; rather, they may require some adjustment to your palate. In the meantime, here are some things to look for when opening up and sampling your pickled items.

INSPECT YOUR PICKLES

Before eating your pickles, you should visually inspect them. Is there any mold growth, or have any other strange changes occurred? If the pickle is in cold storage and there is mold, this is a sure sign that something is wrong, and the pickles should be discarded without tasting.

In some pickles, like sauerkraut, the cabbage will darken during fermentation. This is not a sign of spoilage, but a normal part of the process. If you are in doubt, review the specific troubleshooting guides for pickles and sauerkraut (page 31 and page 59). Likewise, if mold occurs on sauerkraut during fermentation, in some instances this can be removed and the fermentation process can continue. Be sure to review specific recipes and troubleshooting for that item, and immediately take action as needed.

In canned and fresh pickled items, fermentation should not be taking place, meaning there should be no moving bubbles in the jar. If there are, this too is a sign of spoilage, and the food should be disposed of promptly.

USE YOUR OTHER SENSES

Open the jar and smell the pickles. Are there any off odors? Some pickles may be a little more pungent than you are used to eating. However, this does not mean they've gone bad. At the same time, pickles should not smell like they are rotting or any other foul smell associated with decomposition. If this occurs, discard the pickles from any place that animals or humans could consume them.

Another leading indicator of spoilage is sliminess. Pickled foods should not have this texture. If they have, this is likely due to bacterial contamination, and the pickles should be discarded without tasting.

Don't get discouraged if you make a mistake or something goes wrong. These are natural processes and sometimes things just go awry. However, there is no reason to be fearful of your food. As long as you are following recipes and inspecting your pickles, there is little reason for concern when it comes to pickling safety.

3

YOUR FIRST REFRIGERATED DILL PICKLE

You've got all the equipment and are ready to go, so now what? Look no further than this simple refrigerator dill pickle recipe to get you started. A jar, cucumbers, and a few basic ingredients is all you need to get you well on your way to enjoying some delicious, homemade pickles. Check out the following recipe for classic dill pickles that are ready to eat within only a day or two. After all, when it comes to pickling, waiting is the hardest part! For maximum flavor, though, store the pickles in the fridge for up to one week before eating, especially if you plan on leaving the pickles whole.

FROM THE MASTERS

KELLY McVICKER, OWNER & FOUNDER OF McVICKER PICKLES
www.mcvickerpickles.com

I come from several generations of farmers, so there has always been a connection to food and feeding people in my family. But I definitely didn't set out to become a professional pickler. I worked in the women's human rights field for nearly nine years before the office routine got to be too much for my soul. I started digging up and testing old family recipes as a way to balance all that computer time. Before long I was getting up extra early to hit up the farmers' market before work, then spending all evening experimenting with pickles, jams, and anything else I could put in a jar. It all unfolded from there.

I love pickles, but I think what I truly love is the pickling process. There's something so satisfying about it: selecting the produce, preparing the equipment, mixing the spices, chopping, packing, and finally canning the jars in the water bath. If you've done it right, you get to hear the magical 'ping' of a sealed jar, which is music to a canner's ears. I like seeing the whole process through from start to finish.

My advice for people just learning how to pickle? Pay close attention to the process. You can spend hours searching for the perfect recipe, or pestering old ladies at farmers' markets for their secret ingredients, but your time would be better spent learning the steps and understanding why they're important. Pickling has been around since Ancient Egypt, so you're probably not going to discover some secret ingredient or spice blend anyway. It's all about following the process. Start by using the freshest produce you can get your hands on. Leftover veggies from the back of your fridge make bad pickles. Get up early, go to the farmers' market, and make a day of it.

McVicker Pickles is a San Francisco-based company that makes pickles and mustard in small batches. They also offer monthly workshops on food preservation skills including pickling, fermentation, and jam and jelly making. Owner and founder Kelly McVicker did her basic training with her Kansas grandmas Margarett and Harriet, and is now certified as a Master Food Preserver in San Francisco County.

THE PREP

Follow these simple steps to get your pickling project underway:

GATHER THE INGREDIENTS. Before starting, it is best to have everything you need on hand in front of you. Review the recipe, and gather the ingredients to get started.

WASH AND CLEAN THE CUCUMBERS. Cucumbers are grown close to the ground so are notoriously dirty. Give them a good washing before you begin, but not too far ahead of time, as this can promote spoilage. Right before you are planning to make the pickles is the best time. Remove the blossom ends of the cucumbers, as they can cause spoilage as well. (The blossom end is the one opposite the stem. You can either slice this end off with a sharp knife, or scrape it off with your fingernail.)

SLICE THE CUCUMBERS. Depending on the type and size of your cucumbers, you may want to halve them lengthwise, quarter them, or leave them whole. This is completely up to your personal preference. Just make sure that the pieces are relatively uniform in size and will fit nicely in your jars.

PREPARE THE JARS. Wash the jars you will be using in warm, soapy water, and rinse them well. Leave them on the counter to air-dry while preparing the pickles. Depending on the type of pickle, the recipe may call for sterilized jars. If this is the case, the jars should be boiled in water for 10 minutes before using. If the recipe states only "prepared jars," washing them in warm, soapy water is fine.

CUCUMBER VARIETIES FOR PICKLING

AMERICAN PICKLING CUCUMBERS: There are many varieties of American pickling cucumbers available, and American pickling cucumbers are the type most widely sold. They all taste very similar and can be used for most cucumber pickling projects. American pickling cucumbers are generally used when they are in the 3- to 5-inch range; however, smaller cucumbers—about 1 to 2 inches—can also be used for making gherkin-type pickles. Because they are small, they can be left whole or, if desired, cut into spears, sliced, or diced. American pickling cucumbers are easy to grow and can be found in seed catalogs as well as at most garden centers. For more information, see the Resources section (page 160).

ASIAN PICKLING CUCUMBERS: These are a type of cucumber specifically used in Japanese and other Asian pickling projects. Long and nearly seedless, these Asian cucumbers have a slightly different texture and flavor. Their skins are generally thinner than the American varieties, though they still hold up well to various types of pickling. The most common varieties of these include China Hybrid, Orient Express Hybrid, and Suyo long cucumbers. Find these cucumbers in specialty seed catalogs.

MASTER DILL PICKLE RECIPE

MAKES 1 QUART

If you like the pucker of a dill pickle without a long fermentation time, this refrigerator dill recipe is for you. With little prep time you can transform a quart of cucumbers into delicious, crisp dills. The cucumbers need a week to develop their full dill flavor, but they're so delicious after even just a day, you may not be able to wait. The brining step keeps the pickles crisp and is simple to complete, especially if you start the night before.

PREP TIME: 15 minutes, plus 8 to 12 hours brining
COOK TIME: 5 minutes
CURING TIME: 1 week

1¼ pounds pickling cucumbers

3 tablespoons pickling salt, plus 2 teaspoons, divided

4¾ cups water, divided

1 small onion, peeled and quartered

1 garlic clove, peeled

2 dill heads

¾ cup distilled white vinegar or apple cider vinegar

2 tablespoons sugar

1. Wash the cucumbers and remove the blossom ends (see fig. A). Halve or quarter the cucumbers lengthwise depending on their size. Place the cucumbers in a large nonreactive bowl. Mix 3 tablespoons of salt in 4 cups of water, and stir to dissolve. Pour this brine over the cucumbers, and use a plate to hold the cucumbers below the brine. Let sit for 8 to 12 hours, covered by a clean kitchen towel.

2. Drain the cucumbers and rinse them well. Pack the cucumbers into a quart jar along with the onion, garlic, and dill heads (see fig. B).

In a small saucepan, combine the remaining ¾ cup water, vinegar, remaining 2 teaspoons salt, and sugar. Bring the mixture to a boil, stirring until the spices are dissolved (see fig. C). Turn off the heat and pour the hot liquid over the cucumbers (see fig. D). Close the jar and let it sit on the counter until cool.

3. Refrigerate it for 1 week before eating for the best flavor, and store it refrigerated for up to 2 months.

TRY INSTEAD

If you don't grow your own dill or live near a farmers' market, finding fresh dill may be a challenge. If necessary, dill seeds can be substituted for the fresh dill heads. Substitute 1 tablespoon of dill seeds per 2 heads of fresh dill.

STORE YOUR DILL PICKLES

Unless you are canning your pickles to make them shelf stable, they should be stored in the refrigerator once complete. In most cases, they can be stored in the same container in which they were made, closed with a lid. The exception to this is if they were made in a pickling crock. In this case, they should be transferred to a jar covered with a nonreactive lid. Pay attention to storage tips on each individual recipe as they can vary widely according to the type of pickle.

DILL PICKLE TROUBLESHOOTING TIPS

PICKLE PROBLEM	POSSIBLE CAUSE
Soft pickles	• Overheating during processing • Not processed soon enough after picking
Hollow middle	• Inadequate watering while growing (remove these before processing; they float when submerged in water)
Darkened pickles	• Use of reactive metal during processing • Growing soil • Spices • Corrosion on the lids
Shriveled pickles	• Not processed soon enough after picking • Too much salt, vinegar, or sugar • Overheating during processing
Sediment in jar	• Use of table salt

GROWING YOUR OWN CUCUMBERS

Cucumbers are quite easy to grow. Whether you have a large garden or simply a patio with a few pots, consider adding some of these pickling treats to your gardening schedule this year. If you plan on being an avid pickler, here are some distinct reasons that growing your own cucumbers make a good practice:

- **BEST SELECTION:** Unless you live in a farming mecca, chances are your pickling cucumber options available from the market or store will be pretty limited. Growing your own cucumbers for pickling gives you control over which varieties you have to choose from for your pickling projects. Order seeds from any number of specialty retailers featured in Resources (page 160).

- **FRESH IS BEST:** Cucumbers fresh from the field are always your best option for the best pickles. Growing them yourself allows you to know exactly when the cucumbers are picked and enables you to use them straight away in your favorite recipes. Cucumbers should be processed within two days of picking, and only one if they are small—1 to 2 inches—to ensure they do not begin to shrivel.

- **EASY TO GROW:** Once your cucumber plant has taken hold, there is not much to stop its growth. If space is an issue, cucumbers can be trellised up, allowing you to grow them in small spots, including in containers. The most vital issue is that you water the plants regularly, especially once they begin producing cucumbers. If they don't receive sufficient water, the cucumbers will become bitter. As soon as the cucumbers are ready to pick, you can begin making them into small-batch pickles.

THE RECIPES

II

4

FRESH PICKLES

These are some of the easiest pickles to produce. They require little work and deliver big flavor. While the prep work for all of these is rather quick, and they do not require cooking or fermentation, you will need to store some of these pickles for days or weeks before they obtain their full flavor.

Many of these recipes contain information about canning the pickles. Others do not. If you prefer, rather than canning them, cap the pickles with a nonreactive lid and store them in the refrigerator until their flavor is fully developed. If you simply can't wait, begin sampling them a little early for a taste. No one will tell on you if you eat the whole jar, and you'll only have a reason to make more!

QUICK DILL PICKLES

4

Quite possibly one of the easiest canned dill pickle recipes around, these cucumbers require no brining, and are ready to go into the jar for pickling in a flash. For a large harvest, double or triple the recipe, and you'll be glad you did. Invite some friends to help can up a big batch, and you'll have a treasure trove of pickles in no time. Because they can be stored for up to a year, there's no rush to eat them all at once.

PREP TIME: 10 minutes
PROCESSING TIME: 10 minutes for pints,
   15 minutes for quarts
CURING TIME: 1 month

5¼ pounds pickling cucumbers
1 tablespoon black peppercorns
8 dill heads
¼ cup minced garlic cloves
5 tablespoons plus 1 teaspoon pickling salt
3¾ cups white vinegar or apple cider vinegar
4 cups water

1. Wash the cucumbers and remove the blossom ends. Halve, quarter, or leave the cucumbers whole depending on their size.

2. Divide the peppercorns, dill, and garlic between the jars. Pack the cucumbers into the jars snugly.

3. Combine the salt, vinegar, and water in a nonreactive saucepan. Bring to a boil and stir to dissolve the salt. Ladle the liquid over the cucumbers, leaving ½ inch of headspace. Cap the jars with two-piece canning lids.

4. Process the pint jars for 10 minutes and the quart jars for 15 minutes in a boiling-water bath. Store the jars in a dark, cool, dry place for at least 1 month before eating.

TRY INSTEAD

This recipe is highly customizable to your taste. If you prefer, add one or two of your favorite type of chile peppers or another favorite seasoning to your pickles, and see what you think. However, never change the ratio of vinegar to water, as this keeps the pickles safe to consume.

ICICLE PICKLES

MAKES 4 PINTS

Often called sweet pickles, these icicle pickles can be described as a little sweet, along with plenty of sour. To avoid the cloyingly sweet flavor of some varieties of this pickle, this recipe has less sugar than most. But if you like your pickles really sweet, you can increase the sugar, as you prefer. To add some spice to the mix as well, add one or two dried chile peppers per jar.

PREP TIME: 10 minutes, plus 2 to 4 hours soaking
PROCESSING TIME: 10 minutes
CURING TIME: 2 weeks

5¼ pounds pickling cucumbers
1½ pounds shallots, sliced
½ cup pickling salt
4½ cups white vinegar
2½ cups sugar
1 teaspoon ground turmeric
2 teaspoons mustard seeds
½ teaspoon celery seeds

1. Wash the cucumbers and remove the blossom ends. Halve, quarter, or leave the cucumbers whole depending on their size. Toss the cucumbers and shallots with salt and refrigerate, covered, for 2 to 4 hours. Drain the water from the bowl. Pack the cucumbers into prepared pint jars.

2. Combine the remaining ingredients in a non-reactive pot and bring to a boil. Ladle the liquid over the cucumbers, leaving ½ inch of headspace. Cap the jars with two-piece canning lids.

3. Process the pints in a boiling-water bath for 10 minutes. Store the jars in a dark, cool, dry place for at least 2 weeks before eating.

A CLOSER LOOK

Turmeric is a powerful anti-inflammatory and anti-oxidant, and is very easy to include in your diet. An essential ingredient in curry powders, it has an astringent flavor that lies somewhere between ginger and oranges. Note that turmeric is quick to stain clothing with its bright orange hue, so be careful when working with it in your kitchen.

BREAD AND BUTTER PICKLES

Fabulous on a sandwich or burger, these sweet rounds are as versatile as they are delicious. Using less sugar than a typical bread-and-butter pickle recipe, these deliver plenty of flavor and sweetness, without being overwhelmingly sweet.

PREP TIME: 15 minutes, plus 2 to 4 hours soaking
PROCESSING TIME: 10 minutes
CURING TIME: 2 weeks

2 pounds pickling cucumbers
2 tablespoons pickling salt
2 teaspoons mustard seeds
¼ teaspoon celery seeds
½ teaspoon red chili pepper flakes (optional)
1½ cups white vinegar or apple cider vinegar
½ cup water
¼ cup sugar
½ teaspoon ground turmeric

1. Wash the cucumbers and remove the blossom ends. Slice the cucumbers into thin rounds about ¼-inch thick. Toss the cucumbers with the salt and refrigerate, covered, for 2 to 4 hours. Drain the water from the bowl. Toss the cucumbers with the mustard seeds, celery seeds, and red chili pepper flakes, if using. Pack the cucumbers into prepared jars.

2. Combine the vinegar, water, sugar, and turmeric in a nonreactive pot and bring to a boil. Ladle the liquid over the cucumbers, leaving ½ inch of head-space. Cap the jars with two-piece canning lids.

3. Process the pints in a boiling-water bath for 10 minutes. Store the jars in a dark, cool, dry place for at least 2 weeks before eating.

TRY INSTEAD

If you have a bumper crop of zucchini, use it in place of cucumbers for this recipe. When pickled, young zucchini produces nearly the same results as cucumbers. For best results, use young, firm zucchini picked before their seeds become hardened.

JARDINIÈRE

MAKES 2 PINTS

For an avid gardener, this is a fantastic pickle that aptly showcases your harvest. Combining a number of vegetables, jardinière is highly customizable to whatever produce you have on hand, and makes a great addition to an antipasto tray or cold lunch. Use the suggestions here, or substitute your favorite produce in equal proportions to create your own delectable combination.

PREP TIME: 15 minutes
PROCESSING TIME: 20 minutes
CURING TIME: 2 weeks

½ pound onions, peeled and cut into chunks
½ pound carrots, peeled and cut into chunks
½ pound zucchini, cut into thick rounds
½ pound cauliflower florets
1 red or green bell pepper, cut into strips
3 garlic cloves
½ teaspoon black peppercorns
½ teaspoon dried oregano
½ teaspoon dried thyme
2 fresh chile peppers
1 cup water
1½ cups white vinegar
1½ teaspoons pickling salt

1. Divide the vegetables, garlic, peppercorns, oregano, thyme, and chile peppers between the two jars.

2. In a nonreactive pot, combine the water, vinegar, and pickling salt, and bring the liquid to a boil. Ladle the pickling liquid into the jars, leaving ½ inch of headspace. Cap the jars using two-piece canning lids.

3. Process the pints in a boiling-water bath for 20 minutes. Store the jars in a dark, cool, dry place for at least 2 weeks before eating.

PICKLED ARTICHOKE HEARTS

MAKES 1 PINT

Fresh artichokes may be hard to come by if you live in cooler climates, but if you can get your hands on some of these, you will be glad you did. Look for smaller artichokes that enable you to keep the artichoke heart whole in the jars, so you can experience the buttery, smooth taste they exude. Using a combination of lemon juice, vinegar, and olive oil, this is a fresh pickle meant for storing refrigerated. If you can't find fresh, use canned artichokes instead, and skip the first two steps.

PREP TIME: 10 minutes
COOK TIME: 15 minutes
CURING TIME: 1 week

15 baby artichokes
1 lemon, quartered
¼ cup lemon juice
½ cup white vinegar
¼ cup olive oil
1 garlic clove, sliced
1 dried chile pepper
¾ teaspoon salt

1. Pull the leaves off the artichokes until you reach the artichoke heart. Once they are trimmed, drop the artichoke hearts into a nonreactive pot.

2. Squeeze the lemon into the pot with the artichokes, and put the lemon pieces into the pot. Cover with water and bring it to a boil. Cook until the artichokes are fork tender, about 15 minutes.

3. In a nonreactive pot, combine the lemon juice, vinegar, olive oil, garlic clove, chile pepper, and salt. Bring to a boil and simmer for 5 minutes.

4. Pack the artichoke hearts into a jar. Cover with the marinade, leaving ½ inch of headspace. Store the jars in the refrigerator for at least 1 week before eating.

A CLOSER LOOK

When selecting artichokes at the market, look for ones with vibrant green leaves and freshly cut stems. The main crop of artichokes is in the spring, followed by a secondary harvest in the fall. Fall artichokes are frequently characterized by darker or bronzed leaves, and sometimes a whitish, blistered look. This indicates that they were exposed to a light frost, which often heightens their flavors.

PICKLED ASPARAGUS

MAKES 3 (12-OUNCE) JARS

This pickle has become a hot item on supermarket shelves, but you can make it at home rather quickly and for a fraction of the cost. The 12-ounce jelly jars are recommended for this pickle, as they make a great presentation and allow you to pack whole spears uncut thanks to their slightly taller size. Pack the spears either tip up or down, but for the most impressive appearance, be sure to do it uniformly throughout the jar.

PREP TIME: 15 minutes
PROCESSING TIME: 10 minutes
CURING TIME: 2 weeks

2 pounds asparagus, trimmed to fit the jars
4 garlic cloves, crushed
½ teaspoon red chili pepper flakes
½ teaspoon black peppercorns
1½ cups water
1½ cups apple cider vinegar
1 tablespoon sugar
1½ teaspoons pickling salt

1. Bring a large pot of water to a boil and prepare an ice bath by filling a large bowl with equal amounts of water and ice. Add the asparagus to the boiling water, and blanch for 1 minute. Promptly remove the asparagus and transfer to the ice bath until cooled.

2. Divide the garlic, red chili pepper flakes, and peppercorns between the jars. Pack the asparagus into the jars with tips down or up.

3. In a nonreactive pot, combine the water, vinegar, sugar, and pickling salt, and bring to a boil. Ladle the pickling liquid into the jars, leaving ½ inch of headspace. Cap the jars using two-piece canning lids.

4. Process the pints in a boiling-water bath for 10 minutes. Store the jars in a dark, cool, dry place for at least 2 weeks before eating.

TRY INSTEAD

Around the same time of year that asparagus comes to the market, so do garlic scapes, the flowering heads of garlic plants. These mild-tasting spears are similar in texture and appearance to asparagus and make a great pickle as well. Substitute them here for a unique and delicious alternative.

PICKLED BEETS

MAKES 3 PINTS

If you have never tried pickled beets before, now is the time. These sweet, hearty vegetables make a fantastic accompaniment for a number of meals, and are quite affordable. If you buy them with their leaves still on, be sure not to discard them as they are an edible and highly nutritious treat when steamed.

PREP TIME: 45 minutes
PROCESSING TIME: 30 minutes
CURING TIME: 2 weeks

2 pounds red or golden beets
1 (4-inch) cinnamon stick
1 (2-inch) piece ginger, peeled and thinly sliced
½ cup sugar
½ cup brown sugar
2 tablespoons pickling salt
2 cups apple cider vinegar
1 cup water

1. Clean the beets thoroughly. Place them in a large pot, covered with water. Bring the water to a boil and simmer for 20 to 30 minutes, depending on the beet size, until they are tender. Drain and cover with cold water.

2. When the beets are cool enough to handle, slip off their skins. Depending on the size, halve, quarter, or slice the beets.

3. In a nonreactive pot, add the cinnamon stick, ginger, sugar, brown sugar, pickling salt, vinegar, and water. Bring to a boil and simmer for 10 minutes.

4. While simmering, pack the beets into the prepared jars. Ladle the liquid over the beets, leaving ½ inch of headspace. Cap the jars using two-piece canning lids.

5. Process the pints in a boiling-water bath for 30 minutes. Store the jars in a dark, cool, dry place for at least 2 weeks before eating.

A CLOSER LOOK

When purchasing beets, look for ones that are firm and plump. If the greens are attached to the beets, they should be vibrant and leafy. If you buy beets with the greens still attached, remove them from the beets and store them separately, unwashed, in a plastic bag to keep them fresh.

DILLY BEANS

In the height of summer, when beans are at their peak, there is no better time to pickle a few jars (or more) of your favorite variety. Tart and flavorful, these beans are great for snacking, or make a delicious addition to a cold salad.

PREP TIME: 10 minutes
PROCESSING TIME: 5 minutes
CURING TIME: 1 month

1½ pounds young green beans
8 garlic cloves, sliced
4 dill heads
1 teaspoon black peppercorns, crushed
2 cups water
2 cups white vinegar
1 tablespoon pickling salt

1. In sterilized pint jars, pack the green beans snugly. Divide the garlic, dill heads, and peppercorns between the jars.

2. In a nonreactive pot, combine the water, vinegar, and pickling salt. Bring to a boil and promptly ladle the liquid over the beans. Cap the jars using two-piece canning lids.

3. Process the pints in a boiling-water bath for 5 minutes.

4. Store the jars in a dark, cool, dry place for at least 1 month before eating.

A CLOSER LOOK

Bean plants are voracious growers that need very little ground to produce lots of beans. Plant some climbing beans in a large pot or bin in a sunny location, give them something to trellis up, and you'll have plenty of beans for pickling all summer. Try scarlet runner beans, a notoriously quick-growing variety known to be high producers.

SPICY PICKLED BEANS

A different variety of pickled bean altogether, this one focuses almost entirely on turning up the heat. As with any recipe here, you can always scale up or down on the aromatics, such as chile peppers; just be sure to keep the same ratio of vinegar to water. On the other hand, if you prefer to dial the spice up even further, throw a whole chile or two into the jar and see what you think.

PREP TIME: 10 minutes
PROCESSING TIME: 5 minutes
CURING TIME: 1 month

1½ pounds young green beans
4 garlic cloves, sliced
1 teaspoon red chili pepper flakes
1 tablespoon mixed pickling spice
2 cups water
2 cups white vinegar
2 tablespoons pickling salt

1. In three sterilized jars, snugly pack the green beans. Divide the garlic, red chili pepper flakes, and pickling spice between the jars.

2. In a nonreactive pot, mix the water, vinegar, and pickling salt. Bring to a boil and promptly ladle the liquid over the beans. Cap the jars using two-piece canning lids.

3. Process the pints in a boiling-water bath for 5 minutes.

4. Store the jars in a dark, cool, dry place for at least 1 month before eating.

PICKLED CAULIFLOWER

The crunch of cauliflower is preserved in this easy pickle that works equally well on a salad or served on its own as a simple side. Cumin, coriander, and mustard seeds kiss the cauliflower with their notable yet subtle flavors, while a dose of red chili pepper flakes kick things up just enough.

PREP TIME: 10 minutes
PROCESSING TIME: 10 minutes
CURING TIME: 1 month

1 teaspoon cumin seeds

2 teaspoons coriander seeds

1 teaspoon mustard seeds

½ teaspoon red chili pepper flakes

1 (2-pound) cauliflower head, cut into small florets

1½ cups water

2 cups white vinegar

3 tablespoons pickling salt

1. Divide the cumin seeds, coriander seeds, mustard seeds, and red chili pepper flakes between the pint jars. Pack the cauliflower tightly into the jars.

2. In a nonreactive pot, combine the water, vinegar, and pickling salt. Bring to a boil and promptly ladle the liquid over the cauliflower. Cap the jars using two-piece canning lids.

3. Process the pints in a boiling-water bath for 10 minutes.

4. Store the jars in a dark, cool, dry place for at least 1 month before eating.

TRY INSTEAD

Many recipes use white vinegar, due to both its neutral flavor and affordability. However, if you prefer, you can substitute an equal amount of apple cider vinegar in any recipe instead. What's important to remember is that if you are canning the pickle, always use 5 percent acidity vinegar.

4

FRESH PICKLES

PICKLED SWEET PEPPERS

Sweet peppers make for an exceptionally sour, crunchy addition to your salads, dips, or antipasto tray. Simple to prepare using just a few ingredients, these will give you a new way to think about the classic bell pepper. Double or triple the recipe to pickle even more peppers after a big harvest.

PREP TIME: 10 minutes
PROCESSING TIME: 10 minutes
CURING TIME: 2 weeks

2 garlic cloves

2 shallots, sliced

1 pound red, yellow, or green bell peppers, cut into strips

1 cup water

1 cup white vinegar

1 teaspoon pickling salt

½ cup sugar

1. Divide the garlic and shallots between the jars. Place the peppers into the jar so that they fit snugly.

2. In a nonreactive pot, bring the remaining ingredients to a boil. Ladle the liquid into the jars, leaving ½ inch of headspace. Cap the jars with two-piece canning lids.

3. Process for 10 minutes in a boiling-water bath.

4. Store the jars in a cool, dry, dark location for at least 2 weeks before eating.

TRY INSTEAD

For a bit more flavor, add a few jalapeños or Anaheim chiles to the pickled peppers in exchange for some of the bell peppers. Alternatively, you might add a ½ teaspoon of red chili pepper flakes to the mixture.

PICKLED EGGPLANT

MAKES 1 PINT

Even if you have never been a fan of eggplant, you may want to give this vegetable another chance as a pickle. Pickling infuses eggplant with a bold and unique flavor. Eat it as part of an antipasto tray, mix it into salads, or serve it alongside hummus and bread.

PREP TIME: 10 minutes, plus 12 hours resting time
COOK TIME: none
CURING TIME: 3 days

1½ pounds small eggplants, peeled
2 teaspoons pickling salt
½ cup red wine vinegar
3 garlic cloves, sliced
1 tablespoon minced fresh basil leaves
1 teaspoon minced fresh oregano leaves
1 teaspoon red chili pepper flakes
Olive oil, to cure

1. Slice the eggplant into strips. Mix the eggplant strips in a bowl with the salt, place the strips into a colander, and allow them to drain over a bowl for 12 hours.

2. Press the eggplant strips in your clean hands to remove excess moisture. Toss the strips in a bowl with the vinegar.

3. In a pint jar, layer the eggplant with the garlic, basil, oregano, and red chili pepper flakes, pressing down as you go so that all the eggplant fits snugly in the jar.

4. Add enough olive oil to cover the eggplant. Cap the jar using a nonreactive lid, and place the jar in the refrigerator. Check it after several hours to ensure that the olive oil is covering the eggplant. If not, add more until the eggplant is fully covered.

5. Store the jar, refrigerated, for at least 3 days before eating. Serve within 2 weeks.

A CLOSER LOOK

When pickling eggplant, the smaller Chinese or Japanese varieties are the best options. These smaller varieties of eggplant have a firmer texture and better flavor than the larger American variety found in many supermarkets. If you can't find these near you, consider ordering some seeds and growing them yourself. Eggplant is extremely easy to grow, and just one plant will give you a plentiful harvest throughout the growing season.

PICKLED MUSHROOMS

MAKES 1 PINT

Pickled mushrooms require little time to prepare, and can take ordinary mushrooms to new heights. Serve these pickled mushrooms as a side dish, appetizer, or alongside flavorful meats. Use a mix of your favorite mushrooms, or choose just one variety. Either way, try to wait for at least three days before tasting them to allow them to reach their maximum flavor.

PREP TIME: 10 minutes
COOK TIME: 15 minutes
CURING TIME: 3 days

1 pound mixed or single-variety mushrooms (such as cremini, shiitake, enoki, oyster, button)
1 small onion, peeled and chopped
2 bay leaves
2 teaspoons black peppercorns
2 sprigs fresh thyme
1 garlic clove, sliced
½ cup water
½ cup white wine vinegar
2 teaspoons pickling salt
1 teaspoon sugar

1. In a nonreactive pot, combine all the ingredients. Bring to a boil, then reduce the heat and simmer for 15 minutes. Pack the mushrooms and the pickling liquid into a pint jar. Let the jar cool at room temperature.

2. Close the jar with a nonreactive lid, refrigerate, and store for at least 3 days before eating. Once refrigerated, store for up to 3 weeks.

PICKLED HOT PEPPERS

If you enjoy hot pepper rings on your sandwiches or over greens, this recipe is for you. While there is no shortage of pickled hot pepper recipes available for canning, this one is both simple and raw, allowing the peppers to retain much of their crunch. These peppers make a perfect addition to a number of meals that need heating up, and because they are raw, they don't become soggy.

PREP TIME: 10 minutes
COOK TIME: 10 minutes
CURING TIME: 1 week

1 pound hot peppers (jalapeño, Thai, serrano)

2 garlic cloves

2 tablespoons black peppercorns

1½ tablespoons pickling salt

1 tablespoon sugar

¾ cup white vinegar

¾ cup water

1. Slice the peppers into rings, or for smaller peppers, pierce them several times with a skewer and leave them whole. Pack the peppers into a sterile quart jar.

2. In a nonreactive pot, combine the remaining ingredients and bring them to a boil. Reduce the heat and simmer for 10 minutes. Ladle the brine over the peppers and allow them to sit at room temperature until cooled.

3. Cap the jar using a nonreactive lid, and refrigerate for 1 week before eating. Refrigerated, the peppers will keep for up to 8 weeks.

A CLOSER LOOK

Using a mixture of peppers gives you a more complex and flavorful brine and pickle. If you want to keep things mild, you can also substitute banana peppers here, but consider adding a few hotter jalapeños, if only for their unique flavor. When you are done with the peppers, use the brine for flavoring sauces and soups that could use a little heat.

PICKLED GREEN TOMATOES

MAKES 1 PINT

If you've ever grown tomatoes, you surely experienced green tomatoes left over at the end of the growing season. These last tomatoes that don't ripen don't have to be destined for compost. Instead, you can pickle them for a tangy treat any time of the year. For this recipe, be sure to use completely green tomatoes with no hints of color.

PREP TIME: 10 minutes
COOK TIME: 5 minutes
CURING TIME: 1 week

¾ pound green tomatoes
2 cloves garlic
1 head fresh dill
1 teaspoon mixed pickling spice
1¾ cups white vinegar
1¾ cups water
2 tablespoons pickling salt

1. Cut the tomatoes in halves or quarter them, depending on the size.

2. Pack the garlic, dill, and pickling spice, followed by the tomatoes, into the jar.

3. In a nonreactive pot, bring the vinegar, water, and pickling salt to a boil. Ladle the liquid into the jar, leaving ½ inch of headspace. Cap the jar with a nonreactive lid.

4. Store for at least 1 week before eating. Refrigerated, the pickles will keep for up to 2 months.

PICKLED KOHLRABI

MAKES 1 QUART

Kohlrabi is not traditional supermarket fare, but many farmers' markets and specialty stores now carry this member of the cabbage family. If you can't find it, try growing it yourself—it's a hardy plant that's easy to cultivate. With its mild cabbage flavor, the bulbous stem is a treat both raw and cooked. Use a sharp knife to peel, but before peeling, be sure to halve or quarter it—especially if you have a large one—to prevent it from rolling on the cutting board.

PREP TIME: 15 minutes, plus 1 hour resting time
COOK TIME: 5 minutes
CURING TIME: 2 days

3 carrots, peeled and cut into chunks

1½ pounds kohlrabi, peeled and cut into chunks

2 teaspoons pickling salt

4 cloves garlic, chopped

1 cup water

1 cup white vinegar

2 tablespoons sugar

1 (2-inch) piece of ginger, peeled and thinly sliced

¼ teaspoon red chili pepper flakes

¼ teaspoon black peppercorns, coarsely crushed

1. Toss the carrots, kohlrabi, and salt in a bowl, and let the mixture stand for 1 hour. Drain the kohlrabi and carrots, and pack them into a quart jar.

2. Bring the rest of the ingredients to a boil and pour them over the kohlrabi. Cap the jar with a non-reactive lid and allow it to cool to room temperature.

3. Refrigerate and store for 2 days before eating. The kohlrabi will keep for up to 3 weeks refrigerated.

A CLOSER LOOK

Kohlrabi can be eaten both raw and cooked, and works best steamed, baked, braised, or stir-fried. Whatever you choose, be sure not to toss its leafy green leaves. The nutritious leaves have a similar flavor to collards and kale, and keep well refrigerated when separated and stored on their own in a produce bag.

PICKLED GARLIC

MAKES 1 PINT

While peeling the garlic may take considerable time, the effort is well worth it. Lasting up to a year, this pickle is great to have on hand when you are out of fresh garlic, as it can serve as a simple substitute. Then use the vinegar pickling brine to lend extra flavor to dressings and sauces, and you'll be happy you did.

PREP TIME: 30 minutes
COOK TIME: none
CURING TIME: 1 month

2 cups peeled whole garlic cloves
1 cup white vinegar
1 teaspoon sugar
1 teaspoon pickling salt
1 teaspoon black peppercorns, coarsely crushed

1. Pack the garlic into a pint jar.

2. Mix the vinegar, sugar, salt, and peppercorns together in a bowl, stirring to dissolve the sugar and salt. Pour the mixture over the garlic. Cover the jar with a nonreactive lid and refrigerate.

3. Store for 1 month before using, or refrigerate for up to 1 year.

A CLOSER LOOK

Garlic is a powerful antibacterial, antifungal, and anti-carcinogenic food used in natural medicine to treat a number of conditions, including influenza, high blood pressure, and cholesterol, and to improve digestion. Use it liberally in your cooking for both flavor and its health benefits.

PICKLED ONIONS

Pickled onions can bring a salad to life, and provide a great accompaniment to meats, cheeses, and other vegetables. This simple recipe is not for canning, but for a quick pickle you can make as little as 1 hour ahead of serving. Red onions are used here for their mild flavor and bright color that will liven up any plate.

PREP TIME: 5 minutes
COOK TIME: none
CURING TIME: 1 hour

1 cup apple cider vinegar
2 teaspoons pickling salt
2 tablespoons sugar
2 red onions, peeled and sliced

1. In a small bowl, mix the vinegar, salt, and sugar until the salt and sugar are dissolved.

2. Pack the onions into a jar. Pour the liquid over the onions and cap with a nonreactive lid.

3. Refrigerate and store for at least 1 hour before serving. The pickled onions will keep for up to 2 weeks refrigerated.

4

FRESH PICKLES

SIMPLE PICKLED EGGS

Pickled eggs possess an incredibly smooth texture lacking in plain old hard-boiled eggs. Serve them on a salad, or as a quick snack on the go. When using large chicken eggs, a dozen should fit snugly in a quart jar. For a smaller batch, simply cut the recipe in half and use a pint jar instead.

PREP TIME: 10 minutes, plus 30 minutes
    cooling time
COOK TIME: 10 minutes
CURING TIME: 1 week

12 hard-boiled eggs
1 tablespoon pickling salt
1½ cups white vinegar
½ cup water
½ teaspoon crushed black peppercorns
1 tablespoon sugar
1 tablespoon mixed pickling spice

1. Pack the eggs into a quart jar.

2. In a nonreactive pot, bring the remaining ingredients to a boil, reduce the heat, and simmer for 10 minutes. Turn off the heat and cool the brine for 30 minutes, until it reaches room temperature.

3. Ladle the liquid over the eggs, close the jar with a nonreactive lid, and refrigerate.

4. Store for 1 week before eating. The pickled eggs will keep for up to 3 weeks refrigerated.

A CLOSER LOOK

Eggs are a highly perishable food and should never be stored at room temperature. Be careful of this when making pickled eggs, as improperly stored pickled eggs have been known to produce botulism. This is not a risk if you promptly refrigerate your eggs and do not allow them to sit unrefrigerated in the "danger zone" of 40°F to 140°F for more than 2 hours.

SPICY PICKLED EGGS

For those who like to turn up the heat, this pickled egg recipe is a great place to start. Featuring a medley of peppers, this colorful combination endows the eggs with a serious kick of spice. Pickled eggs pair well with an ice-cold beer, and this spicy version will not disappoint.

PREP TIME: 10 minutes, plus 30 minutes
  cooling time
COOK TIME: 10 minutes
CURING TIME: 2 days

12 hard-boiled eggs

1½ cups white vinegar

½ cup water

¼ cup sugar

1 red bell pepper, sliced

3 habanero peppers, sliced

3 jalapeño peppers, sliced

2 teaspoons pickling salt

1 tablespoon mixed pickling spice

2 teaspoons red chili pepper flakes

6 whole cloves

1. Pack the eggs into a quart jar.

2. Bring all the other ingredients to a boil, reduce the heat, and simmer for 10 minutes. Turn off the heat and let the brine cool to room temperature, for 30 minutes. Ladle over the eggs, cap with a non-reactive lid, and refrigerate.

3. Store for 2 days before eating. These pickled eggs will keep for up to 3 weeks refrigerated.

5
FERMENTED PICKLES

Fermented pickles are fun to make, and can satisfy your inner scientist. Combining science and art, these projects for producing masterful probiotic pickles are ready for your own interpretation. These diverse living foods span a wide range of tastes. Using mason jars and a few widely available ingredients, you can turn your garden produce into creations that both improve your health and add vibrant flavor to your meals.

SAUERKRAUT

MAKES 1 QUART

This sauerkraut is a basic recipe to get you started in fermentation. Choose between caraway seeds and juniper berries to add some extra flavor, or simply leave them out. Depending on the temperature of the location where you ferment the cabbage, the amount of time it requires can vary considerably. For the best flavor (and longest fermentation time) aim for a location that maintains a temperature of around 60°F to 70°F.

PREP TIME: 15 minutes, plus 1 hour resting time
FERMENTATION TIME: 2 to 6 weeks

2 pounds cabbage, shredded
4 teaspoons pickling salt
1 teaspoon caraway seeds or juniper berries (optional)

1. Prepare the cabbage by first removing the inner core. Split the cabbage into quarters and thinly slice using a sharp knife or mandolin. Cut the cabbage into shreds about ¼-inch thick (see fig. A).

2. In a large nonreactive bowl, mix the cabbage and salt. Massage the salt gently into the cabbage (see fig. B). Leave the cabbage at room temperature for an hour to allow it to release some of its juices.

3. Add the caraway seeds or juniper berries, if using, and mix well.

4. Pack the cabbage into a quart jar, tamping it down with a smaller jar or your fist as you go, and add any juices from the bowl (see fig. C).

5. Apply a weight and close the jar using a nonreactive lid. Set the jar in a cool location (see fig. D).

6. After 1 day, check the sauerkraut to make sure that it is covered in its brine. If it isn't, add brine by mixing 1 cup of water with 1 teaspoon of salt and pouring over the sauerkraut until it is covered. Reapply the weight and place the jar in a cool location.

7. Check the sauerkraut daily to ensure it remains submerged in its brine and that no scum appears. If scum appears on the surface, skim it off promptly, rinse the weight off, and reapply the weight. You will know fermentation has begun when tiny bubbles begin rising to the surface.

8. After 2 weeks, begin tasting the sauerkraut. If it is soured to your liking, place it in the refrigerator at this time. If it isn't, continue with fermentation until you are satisfied with the flavor. Fully fermented sauerkraut will be a light golden color and taste tart.

9. Once fermentation is complete, transfer the sauerkraut to the refrigerator. It can be eaten immediately, but it will continue to cure for the next month and the flavor will develop further. Refrigerated, the sauerkraut will keep several months.

A CLOSER LOOK

Freshly picked cabbage is the best choice when making sauerkraut, as it will be the juiciest and most likely will not require the addition of brine. Find freshly picked cabbage in the fall from a produce market or direct from the farm. Older cabbage can also be used, but because it is drier, the addition of brine is typically necessary.

SAUERKRAUT TROUBLESHOOTING

Because sauerkraut ferments for an extended period, a number of issues may arise. Here are some of the most common, along with what to do should they occur:

- **WHITE SCUM:** Scum on the top of sauerkraut occurs due to the yeast growing because oxygen is not excluded during fermentation. Be sure to keep the sauerkraut below the brine, and skim off scum daily.

- **MOLDY OR ROTTEN KRAUT:** This can happen when the sauerkraut is not held below the brine, or when the fermentation temperature is too high. In either case, simply remove the affected kraut.

- **DARKENED KRAUT:** Sauerkraut darkens when it is exposed to oxygen, when the salting is uneven, or fermentation temperatures are too high. Just remove the darkened kraut.

- **PINK KRAUT:** Sauerkraut can become pink due to yeast growth. This takes place when not weighted properly, too much salt is used, or uneven salting has occurred. Simply discard the pink kraut.

- **SLIMINESS:** Sliminess in fermented foods is never a good thing, and indicates bacterial spoilage. Toss the batch of kraut.

LOADED SAUERKRAUT

There is no reason to stop at classic sauerkraut. Possible additions are pretty much endless, and this loaded version is sure to please. The combination here of cabbage, onions, garlic, and turnips creates a spicy, tart flavor that will have you sneaking forkfuls straight out of the jar.

PREP TIME: 15 minutes, plus 1 hour resting time
FERMENTATION TIME: 2 to 6 weeks

1½ pounds cabbage, shredded
1 onion, peeled, halved, and thinly sliced
6 cloves garlic, minced
2 medium turnips, peeled, halved, and thinly sliced
4 teaspoons pickling salt

1. In a large nonreactive bowl, mix all the ingredients. Let the mixture rest at room temperature for an hour to allow the juices to begin loosening up the cabbage and vegetables.

2. Pack the cabbage and vegetables into a quart jar, using your fist to tamp them down as you go. Apply a weight and close the jar using a nonreactive lid. Set the jar in a cool location.

3. After 1 day, check the sauerkraut to ensure that it is covered in its brine. If it isn't, add brine by mixing 1 cup of water with 1 teaspoon of salt and pouring over the sauerkraut until it is covered. Reapply the weight and place the jar in a cool location.

4. Check the sauerkraut daily to ensure it remains submerged in its brine and that no scum appears. If scum appears on the surface, skim it off promptly, rinse the weight off, and reapply the weight. You will know fermentation has begun when tiny bubbles begin rising to the surface.

5. Ferment the sauerkraut for 2 to 6 weeks. After 2 weeks, begin tasting the sauerkraut. If it is soured to your liking, place it in the refrigerator at this time. If not, continue with fermentation until you are satisfied with the flavor.

6. Once fermentation is complete, transfer the sauerkraut to the refrigerator. It can be eaten immediately, but it will continue to cure for the next month and the flavor will develop further. Refrigerated, the sauerkraut will last several months.

A CLOSER LOOK

Traditionally, sauerkraut is fermented in the fall when temperatures are cooler, making for a longer fermentation time. At 70°F to 75°F, fermentation takes anywhere from 2 to 4 weeks, while at 60°F it can take as long as 6 weeks. Regardless of temperature, the easiest indicator that fermentation is complete is that the tiny bubbles that signal fermentation is taking place will stop rising to the surface.

KALE KRAUT

Any type of green can be fermented, and the process improves the availability of nutrients for your body to absorb. This alternative kraut features kale, a dark leafy green available in many varieties at most stores. For the easiest preparation, use baby kale, which requires no prep work as the stems are edible when thin. If you prefer the larger leaves, simply remove the thick stems before fermenting.

PREP TIME: 15 minutes
FERMENTATION TIME: 2 to 4 days
CURING TIME: 3 to 5 days

15 cups tightly packed kale leaves
2 cloves garlic, minced
1 tablespoon pickling salt
2 wedges of lemon

1. Prepare the kale by stacking several leaves at a time, rolling them up, and then thinly slicing them into strips. As you work, transfer the kale to a large bowl. If you are using baby kale, you can choose whether to shred the kale or leave the leaves whole.

2. Add the garlic and salt to the bowl and mix thoroughly.

3. Pack the kale into a quart jar, tucking the lemon wedges into the top. Cover the jar with a nonreactive lid and leave at room temperature for 2 to 4 days. Transfer the kale to the refrigerator, where its flavors will mellow over 3 to 5 days. Refrigerated, this kraut will keep for 2 weeks.

TRY INSTEAD

If salt is an issue in your diet, you can cut the quantity of salt back to 1½ teaspoons, and add about a ¼ cup of kombucha (non-pasteurized) or whey to the ferment to quickly get the process underway.

5

FERMENTED PICKLES

PAPAYA KRAUT

MAKES 1 QUART

FERMENTED PICKLES

5

If you're a fan of Thai papaya salad, you will love this papaya kraut. This is made using green papaya, a hard, crisp, unripe version of the papaya, which you will most likely need to source from an Asian grocery store. Lemongrass and ginger give this alternative sauerkraut its Southeast Asian feel.

PREP TIME: 20 minutes
FERMENTATION TIME: 5 to 7 days

3 pounds green papaya
2 tablespoons pickling salt
2 tablespoons finely chopped lemongrass
1 tablespoon peeled and grated ginger

1. Using a sharp knife, cut the papaya in half, peel with a vegetable peeler, and remove the seeds with a spoon. Shred the papaya with a grater, mandolin, or food processor, and place in a large bowl.

2. Add the remaining ingredients and mix thoroughly. Pack into a quart or 2-quart jar, pressing the papaya down as you go.

3. Weight the papaya and cover the container with a nonreactive lid or clean kitchen towel. Leave the jar to sit in a cool location around 68°F. The following day, the papaya should be covered in its brine. If it isn't, add brine by mixing 1 teaspoon salt in 1 cup of water and pouring it over the papaya until it is covered.

4. Leave at room temperature, with the papaya weighted down below the brine, for 5 to 7 days until soured to your liking. Transfer the papaya to the refrigerator, where it will keep for several weeks.

A CLOSER LOOK

When immature, a green papaya has white seeds. These seeds are edible and can be added to the papaya kraut for additional texture. The seeds contain the enzyme papain, which is a powerful digestive aid.

CLASSIC DILL PICKLES

MAKES 1 QUART

While it may seem daunting to the uninitiated, making fermented dill pickles is actually a pretty simple process, requiring only a few ingredients. When made in a quart jar, there is no need for fancy fermentation equipment: your fermenting vessel doubles as a ready-made storage container, streamlining the entire process. You want to choose a room temperature location around 70°F for fermenting, so try to move the pickles a little ways from the kitchen to maintain a steady temperature and prevent spikes. However, be sure to place your pickles somewhere highly visible, so you can keep an eye on them throughout the process, as they need daily tending.

PREP TIME: 10 minutes
FERMENTATION TIME: 2 to 3 weeks

1½ pounds pickling cucumbers
1 dill head, plus a few additional fronds
4 black peppercorns
1 chile pepper, slit lengthwise
2 tablespoons pickling salt

1. Wash the cucumbers and remove the blossom ends.

2. Pack the dill, peppercorns, and chile pepper into the jar and then add the cucumbers to the jar. Mix the salt with 3 cups water and pour this brine over the pickles.

3. Use a weight to keep the cucumbers submerged, or pour the remaining brine into a zippered freezer bag, seal, and pack it into the mouth of the jar as a weight. Leave the jar at room temperature.

4. After a day or two, bubbles should begin to form and rise in the jar, signaling fermentation. Watch the jar every day, and if any scum appears on the surface of the pickles, skim it off and rinse off the weight. Repack the weight into the mouth of the jar and continue fermentation.

5. The pickles will be ready in 2 to 3 weeks. Test them at about 2 weeks by removing a pickle with a clean utensil and cutting off a small piece for a taste. If it tastes good, they are done. If it's not yet to your liking, return the weight to the mouth of the jar and continue fermentation for up to another week.

6. When fermentation is complete, if you are using a brine bag, discard it. Cap the jar with a nonreactive lid, and transfer it to the refrigerator where the pickles will keep for about 1 month.

A CLOSER LOOK
When pickles have finished fermenting, their color will be a uniform olive-green. Also, the bubbles signaling the start of fermentation will stop rising in the jar.

SPICY DILL PICKLES

MAKES 1 QUART

If you enjoy spicy foods, there is no reason not to enjoy spicy pickles as well. Using a combination of pickling spice, and dried and fresh chile peppers, this is a complex-flavored pickle that goes exceptionally well with a Bloody Mary (page 147) or a handful of pretzels for a simple snack. For a crisp, lightly fermented pickle, stop fermentation on day 10, or continue fermenting until completely soured at about 3 weeks.

PREP TIME: 10 minutes
FERMENTATION TIME: 10 days to 3 weeks

1½ pounds pickling cucumbers
3 chile peppers, slit lengthwise
2 fresh jalapeños, slit lengthwise
2 garlic cloves, crushed
1 teaspoon mixed pickling spice
1 dill head, plus a few additional fronds
2 tablespoons pickling salt

1. Wash the cucumbers and remove the blossom ends.

2. Pack the chile peppers, jalapeño peppers, garlic, pickling spice, and dill into the jar, followed by the cucumbers. Mix the salt with 3 cups water and pour this brine over the pickles.

3. Use a weight to keep the cucumbers submerged, or pour the remaining brine into a zippered freezer bag, seal the bag, and pack it into the mouth of the jar as a weight. Leave the jar at room temperature.

4. After a day or two, bubbles should begin to form and rise in the jar, signaling fermentation. Watch the jar every day, and if any scum appears on the surface of the pickles, skim it off and rinse off the weight. Repack the weight into the mouth of the jar and continue fermentation.

5. The pickles will be ready in 10 days to 3 weeks. Test them at about 10 days by removing a pickle with a clean utensil and cutting off a small piece for a taste before returning it. If it tastes good, they are done. If it's not yet to your liking, return the weight to the mouth of the jar and continue fermentation for up to another week.

6. When fermentation is complete, if you are using a brine bag, discard it. Cap the jar with a nonreactive lid, and transfer it to the refrigerator where the pickles will keep for about 1 month.

A CLOSER LOOK

The use of a brine bag is a great way to keep fermented pickles submerged in the brine and lock out air. Depending on where you place the jar, you may want to put a small plate underneath to collect any brine that seeps over the jar's edges.

GARLIC DILL PICKLES

MAKES 1 QUART

Garlic adds both a hint of spiciness and a soothing, warming flavor to pickles. This version piles the garlic on thick, so you are not only eating a probiotic treat, but providing your body with antibacterial benefits as well.

PREP TIME: 10 minutes
FERMENTATION TIME: 2 to 3 weeks

1½ pounds pickling cucumbers
1 dill head, plus a few additional fronds
¼ cup crushed garlic cloves
2 tablespoons pickling salt

1. Wash the cucumbers and remove the blossom ends.

2. Pack the dill and garlic into the jar, followed by the cucumbers. Mix the salt with 3 cups water and pour this brine over the pickles.

3. Use a weight to keep the cucumbers submerged, or pour the remaining brine into a zippered freezer bag, seal the bag, and pack it into the mouth of the jar as a weight. Leave the jar at room temperature.

4. After a day or two, bubbles should begin to form and rise in the jar, signaling fermentation. Watch the jar every day, and if any scum appears on the surface of the pickles, skim it off and rinse off the weight. Repack the weight into the mouth of the jar and continue fermentation.

5. The pickles will be ready in 2 to 3 weeks. Test a pickle at about 2 weeks by removing a pickle with a clean utensil and cutting off a small piece for a taste before returning it. If it tastes good, the pickles are done. If they're not yet to your liking, return the weight to the mouth of the jar and continue fermentation for up to another week.

6. When fermentation is complete, if you are using a brine bag, discard it. Cap the jar with a nonreactive lid and transfer it to the refrigerator where the pickles will keep for about 1 month.

A CLOSER LOOK

When fermenting and pickling, sanitation is important. Therefore, when removing a brine bag, be sure to place it on a clean plate instead of a counter to prevent contamination. Similarly, never reach into a ferment with your fingers, as this can introduce bacteria. Instead, always use a clean utensil.

INDIAN-INSPIRED PICKLES

MAKES 1 QUART

Fenugreek, cumin, and ginger infuse these pickles with a savory Indian flavor, while turmeric adds its own pungent touch. If possible, opt for fresh turmeric, which has a more intense flavor. It can be found at many Asian supermarkets, as well as natural health food stores.

PREP TIME: 10 minutes
FERMENTATION TIME: 2 to 3 weeks

1½ pounds pickling cucumbers

1 teaspoon cumin seeds

½ teaspoon fenugreek seeds

2 dried chiles

1 (1-inch) piece of ginger, peeled

1 (1-inch) piece of turmeric or ½ teaspoon ground turmeric

2 tablespoons pickling salt

1. Wash the cucumbers and remove the blossom ends.

2. Pack the cumin seeds, fenugreek seeds, chiles, ginger, and turmeric into the jar, followed by the cucumbers. Mix the salt with 3 cups water and pour this brine over the pickles.

3. Use a weight to keep the cucumbers submerged, or pour the remaining brine into a zippered freezer bag, seal the bag, and pack it into the mouth of the jar as a weight. Leave the jar at room temperature.

4. After a day or two, bubbles should begin to form and rise in the jar, signaling fermentation. Watch the jar every day, and if any scum appears on the surface of the pickles, skim it off and rinse off the weight. Repack the weight into the mouth of the jar and continue fermentation.

5. The pickles will be ready in 2 to 3 weeks. Test them at about 2 weeks by removing a pickle with a clean utensil and cutting off a small piece for a taste before returning it. If it tastes good, they are done. If they're not yet to your liking, return the weight to the mouth of the jar, and continue fermentation for up to another week.

6. When fermentation is complete, if you are using a brine bag, discard it. Cap the jar with a nonreactive lid and transfer it to the refrigerator where the pickles will keep for about 1 month.

LACTO-FERMENTED GINGER CARROTS

Fermenting carrots makes snack time fun, especially for kids. These are kid-tested and approved, and sure beat the price for the same thing at trendy stores and farmers' markets. The recipe here calls for carrot sticks, but you can also use shredded carrots or discs; just be sure to taste the carrots and adjust the fermenting time as you go, based on the carrots' thickness.

PREP TIME: 10 minutes
FERMENTATION TIME: 7 to 14 days

1 (2-inch) piece of ginger, peeled and cut into matchsticks

1 pound carrots, peeled and cut into sticks about 4- to 6-inches long

1 tablespoon plus 1 teaspoon pickling salt

3 cups water

1. Pack the ginger into the jar and add the carrots, packing them in snugly. In a bowl or measuring cup, mix the salt and water until the salt is dissolved, and pour the brine over the carrots. Use a weight to keep the carrots submerged in the brine. Cover the jar using a nonreactive lid and leave the jar at room temperature.

2. The carrots will be ready in 7 to 14 days. Test them at around 7 days by removing a stick with a clean utensil and cutting off a small piece for a taste before returning it. If it tastes good, they are done. If they're not yet to your liking, reapply the weight to the carrots and continue fermentation for up to another week.

3. When fermentation is complete, remove the weight and cap the jar with a nonreactive lid. Transfer the jar to the refrigerator where the carrots will keep for at least 2 weeks.

A CLOSER LOOK

If you are short on prep time, you'll find many types of precut carrots in the refrigerator section of most grocery stores. Choose from shredded, chipped, and stick carrots to cut your prep time in half.

IS MY FERMENT DONE?

Many recipes using fermentation provide a wide range for fermentation time. This is because fermentation times vary based on a number of factors, including temperature during fermentation, personal preference, and ingredients used.

To determine if your ferment is complete, here are a couple of items to consider:

- **THE TEXTURE:** Many people like really crisp pickles, while others are drawn to the intense flavor of a more aged pickle. If you prefer your pickles ultra-crisp, you will want to begin checking your pickles on the lower end of the time range. Likewise, if you favor a softer pickle, a longer fermentation time is for you. Additionally, dense produce like carrots, broccoli, radishes, beets, and cabbage take longer to ferment than softer produce such as eggplant, beans, and fruits.

- **THE FLAVOR:** If you want really intense pickles, you are probably going to want to max out the fermentation time, while a shorter fermentation time will mean a less pickled flavor. This is a personal distinction, and you can make this call when you test the pickles yourself.

Test your pickles as you go, using a clean utensil to remove the pickle from the jar. The answer to when they are ready is simply when you think they taste good. Trust your own taste buds and let them make the decision for you.

LACTO-FERMENTED ASPARAGUS

MAKES 1 QUART

One of the first vegetables to become available in spring, asparagus turns out to be an amazing pickled product. It maintains a good crunch when fermented up to two weeks, and is a whole lot cheaper than commercial varieties. Look for fresh asparagus at farmers' markets or your local grocery store to make a quick batch, and you'll be hooked. If you don't have any brine from other vegetables on hand, simply substitute an additional 1 tablespoon of salt instead.

PREP TIME: 10 minutes
FERMENTATION TIME: 10 to 14 days

1 pound asparagus, trimmed to at least 1-inch shorter than the jar
6 garlic cloves, crushed
1 teaspoon black peppercorns
½ teaspoon mixed pickling spice
½ cup fermented vegetable brine
1½ cups water
1 tablespoon pickling salt

1. Wash and dry the asparagus. Pack the garlic cloves, peppercorns, and mixed pickling spice into the jar. Fit the asparagus snugly in the jar, tips all either up or down, leaving about 1 inch of headspace.

2. Pour the vegetable brine over the asparagus. In a small bowl, mix the water and salt until the salt is dissolved. Pour this over the asparagus to cover it. If it is not covered, add a little more water until it is. If necessary, add a weight to hold the asparagus submerged in the brine. Cover the jar with a nonreactive lid and leave the jar in a room temperature location.

3. After a day or two, bubbles should begin to form and rise in the jar, signaling fermentation. Watch the jar every day, and if any scum appears on the surface of the brine, skim it off and rinse off the weight. Repack the weight into the mouth of the jar and continue fermentation.

4. Test the asparagus after 5 days by removing a piece with a clean utensil and cutting off a small slice for a taste before returning it. If it tastes good, it's done. If they're not yet to your liking, return the weight to the mouth of the jar and continue fermentation for up to 14 days total.

5. When fermentation is complete, remove the weight, cap the jar with a nonreactive lid, and transfer it to the refrigerator where the spears will keep for about 1 month.

A CLOSER LOOK

The woody stems of asparagus should be removed before preparing this recipe. Bend each stalk near the bottom and the woody part will snap right off.

LACTO-FERMENTED RADISHES

MAKES 1 QUART

If you like the crunch of a fresh radish, not to worry: it won't get lost in the process of fermentation. These root vegetables maintain their crispness and become milder as they ferment to complete sourness. Choose red globe radishes, or find multi-colored and oblong-shaped ones at farmers' markets in the height of summer.

PREP TIME: 10 minutes
FERMENTATION TIME: 5 to 10 days

1½ pounds radishes, sliced
2 cups water
1½ tablespoons pickling salt

1. Pack the radishes into a quart jar. Mix the water and salt together, stirring until it dissolves. Pour the brine over the radishes. Weight the radishes with a jelly jar or other weight to submerge all of the radishes in the brine. Leave the jar at room temperature.

2. After 5 days, check the radishes for taste. If it tastes good, it's done. If you're not satisfied yet with their flavor, reapply the weight and return them to the counter to ferment for up to 10 days total.

3. When fermentation is complete, remove the weight, cap the jar with a nonreactive lid, and transfer it to the refrigerator where the radishes will keep for about 1 month.

LACTO-FERMENTED BEANS

When the summer is in full swing, it can be hard to keep up with a harvest of beans from your garden. Here is yet another way to keep things under control by grabbing a pound and tossing them in a jar to ferment. Garlic and dill are combined here for a dilly flavored bean; however, feel free to add your favorite herbs or spices to create a fermented bean flavored to your own personal taste. Use tender, young beans for the best results.

PREP TIME: 10 minutes
FERMENTATION TIME: 1 to 2 weeks

½ pound green beans

2 dill heads

4 cloves garlic, crushed

½ teaspoon black peppercorns, crushed

3 cups water

2 tablespoons pickling salt

1. Layer the beans, dill, garlic, and peppercorns in a quart jar. In a small bowl, mix together the water and salt, stirring until the salt is dissolved. Pour the brine over the beans, using a weight to hold the beans below the brine, if needed.

2. After 7 days, check the beans for taste. If they are to your liking, they are done. If you're not yet satisfied with their flavor, reapply the weight and return them to the counter to ferment for up to 14 days total.

3. When fermentation is complete, remove the weight, cap the jar with a nonreactive lid, and transfer it to the refrigerator where the beans will keep for about 1 month.

A CLOSER LOOK

When pickling beans, choose ones that are thin and young as they will pickle more quickly and be the most tender. Avoid string beans that require additional prep; rather, choose a variety of snap beans from the store, or grow your own.

MIXED GARDEN PICKLES

MAKES 2 QUARTS

Mixed garden pickles make use of several kinds of produce, offering a good solution for an overwhelming bounty of summer vegetables. They look great in a jar and are fun to eat, as each item develops its own unique flavor. Make this in a half-gallon jar, or adjust the recipe to the amount of produce you have on hand.

PREP TIME: 10 minutes
FERMENTATION TIME: 2 to 3 weeks

1 to 2 heads cauliflower, separated into florets
1 bell pepper, cut into strips
½ pound green beans
1 onion, peeled and sliced
1 cup carrots, peeled and cut into ½-inch rounds
4 cloves garlic, crushed
1 thyme sprig
½ teaspoon crushed black peppercorns
4 tablespoons pickling salt
6 cups water
1 tablespoon red wine vinegar

1. In a large bowl, toss all the vegetables together. Pack the vegetables into a jar and add the garlic, thyme, and peppercorns. Prepare the brine by dissolving the salt in the water, and pour it over the vegetables. Add the vinegar.

2. Weigh the vegetables down below the brine using a small weight inserted into the mouth of the jar, or use a zippered plastic bag filled with the remaining brine, and insert this into the mouth of the jar. Leave the jar at room temperature.

3. Fermentation should be noticeable after 3 to 5 days, as bubbles will form in the jar. Check the jar daily, and if any scum appears on the surface, skim it off immediately, clean the weight, and add it back to the jar.

4. Check the pickles for doneness after about 2 weeks. If they are soured to your liking, they are ready. If not, add the weight back to the jar and continue to ferment for 3 weeks total. When fermentation is complete, remove the weight, cover with a nonreactive lid, and refrigerate. These pickles will keep for over 1 month.

TRY INSTEAD

Fermentation recipes are highly customizable to your own tastes. In this recipe, it is perfectly fine to swap out any other garden produce. Zucchini, summer squash, eggplant, peas, and broccoli can all be added or substituted. Also, you can swap out the thyme for basil, oregano, or chiles for alternative flavor accents.

DILLY MIXED GARDEN PICKLES

MAKES 2 QUARTS

Adding cabbage to the pickling mix, this mixed pickle delivers a strong dill and lemon flavor, with a little spice to keep things interesting. The fermentation time is up to 3 weeks, but start tasting this as early as 1 week in to check how the flavors are developing—you may enjoy the younger pickle, which has a stronger taste of lemon.

PREP TIME: 10 minutes
FERMENTATION TIME: 1 to 3 weeks

2 cups whole small sweet peppers
2 cups pickling cucumbers, cut into 1-inch rounds
2 cups carrots, peeled and cut into 1-inch rounds
2 cups thinly sliced cabbage
1 cup green beans, cut in half
4 cloves garlic, crushed
2 dill heads
½ teaspoon crushed black peppercorns
½ teaspoon red chili pepper flakes
1 lemon, sliced
1½ tablespoons pickling salt
2 cups water
¼ cup white vinegar

1. In a large bowl, toss all the vegetables together. Pack the vegetables into a jar, layering in the garlic, dill, peppercorns, chili flakes, and lemon. Prepare the brine by dissolving the salt in the water, and pour it over the vegetables. Add the vinegar.

2. Weigh the vegetables down below the brine using a small weight inserted into the mouth of the jar, or use a zippered plastic bag filled with the remaining brine, and insert this into the mouth of the jar. Leave the jar at room temperature.

3. Fermentation should be noticeable after 3 to 5 days, as bubbles will form in the jar. Check the jar daily, and if any scum appears on the surface, skim it off immediately, clean the weight, and add it back to the jar.

4. Check the pickles for doneness after about 1 week. If they are soured to your liking, they are ready. If not, add the weight back to the jar and continue to ferment for 3 weeks total. When fermentation is complete, remove the weight, cover with a nonreactive lid, and refrigerate. These pickles will keep for several months.

LACTO-FERMENTED TURNIPS AND BEETS

MAKES 1 QUART

These turnips are fermented shredded, quite similarly to sauerkraut. Here a beet or two gives the whole ferment its lovely pink hue. While grating with a traditional grater can be tedious, the job is made exceedingly quick using a food processor. If you have one, pull it out to quickly shred the turnips and beets, and they'll be ready for fermentation in no time.

PREP TIME: 10 minutes
FERMENTATION TIME: 2 to 6 weeks

2 pounds turnips, peeled and shredded
½ pound beets, peeled and shredded
1½ tablespoons salt

1. In a large bowl, toss the turnips and beets. Add the salt and mix well. Pack the turnips and beets into a quart jar. Add a weight to the turnip-beet mixture by inserting a jelly jar or other weight into the mouth of the jar. Place a nonreactive lid loosely on the jar, and set the jar in a location between 60°F to 75°F.

2. The following day, check to see that the turnip-beet mixture is submerged in the brine. If not, mix 2½ teaspoons pickling salt with 2 cups of water and add to the jar. Reapply the weight and lid and return the jar to its location.

3. Check the ferment daily for scum on its surface; if it does appear, skim it off and rinse the weights before adding them back to the jar.

4. After 2 weeks, check the turnips for taste. If they are to your liking, they are done. If you are not yet satisfied, reapply the weight and return them to the counter to ferment for up to 6 weeks total, checking for doneness every couple of days.

5. When fermentation is complete, remove the weight, cap the jar with a nonreactive lid, and transfer it to the refrigerator where the turnips will keep for more than 1 month.

PAIR WITH

Pickled turnips make a great addition of flavor and color to a green salad. Serve a generous portion, along with carrots, lettuce, scallions, slivered almonds, and feta cheese, and you have a delicious and filling meal.

LACTO-FERMENTED DAIKON

MAKES 1 QUART

Daikon is a formidable vegetable, both large in size and possibilities. It's actually a rather bland radish on its own, so pickling daikon is one of the most popular ways to eat it, and lacto-fermentation is just the thing to add a bit of probiotic power to your mealtime. This quick ferment can be ready in just days.

PREP TIME: 10 minutes
FERMENTATION TIME: 2 to 3 days

1 pound daikon
4 dried chile peppers
1 (2-inch) piece of ginger, peeled and sliced
2 cups water
1½ tablespoons pickling salt

1. Cut the daikon in half lengthwise and then slice each half into ½-inch-thick half moons. Layer the daikon in a jar along with the chile peppers and ginger. Mix the water and salt until the salt is dissolved, and pour the brine over the daikon until it is covered. Weigh the daikon down with a small weight inserted into the mouth of the jar. Cap the jar loosely with a nonreactive lid, and leave the jar at room temperature to ferment.

2. The daikon will be complete after 2 to 3 days. When you are satisfied with the sourness of the pickle, remove the weight, cap the jar with a nonreactive lid, and transfer it to the refrigerator where the daikon will keep for about 1 month.

SPICY LACTO-FERMENTED OKRA

MAKES 1 QUART

You can't take the sliminess out of okra, so don't expect that. But if you like okra, this spicy pickled version delivers on flavor to create a firm, crisp pickle loaded with umami. If you are a fan of this Southern specialty, try this version and see what you think.

PREP TIME: 15 minutes
FERMENTATION TIME: 7 to 14 days

¾ pound okra
2 banana peppers, cored, seeded, and sliced
2 jalapeño peppers, cored, seeded, and sliced
1 onion, peeled and cut into 8 to 10 wedges
1 head garlic, cloves separated and peeled
2 tablespoons pickling salt
3 cups water

1. Trim the bottoms of the okra and pack them into a quart jar, layering with the peppers, onion, and garlic. Mix the salt with the water until the salt is dissolved. Pour the brine over the okra, weigh the okra down in the jar, and cap the jar loosely with a nonreactive lid. Leave the jar at room temperature.

2. Fermentation should be noticeable after 3 to 5 days, as bubbles will form in the jar. Check the jar daily and if any scum appears on the surface, skim it off immediately, clean the weights, and add it back to the jar.

3. After 7 days, check the okra for taste. If it is to your liking, it is done. If it is not yet to your taste, reapply the weight and return the jar to the counter to ferment for up to 14 days total.

4. When fermentation is finished, remove the weight, cap the jar with a nonreactive lid, and transfer it to the refrigerator where the okra will keep for about 1 month.

A CLOSER LOOK

Okra is high in B-complex vitamins and vitamin C, as well as carotene. It is at its peak in the middle of the summer into the fall. When selecting okra for pickling, look for short pieces, less than 7 inches long, as these are the most tender. Do not store the okra for more two days before pickling.

LACTO-FERMENTED EGGPLANT

MAKES 1 PINT

Fermented eggplant has a different texture entirely from other preparations. If you think of eggplant as a mushy mess, you should try this once to see what you are missing. Soaking up the flavor of the brine, these pickles turn out so great you can eat them by the forkful.

PREP TIME: 10 minutes
FERMENTATION TIME: 7 days

4 small Japanese or other Asian-variety eggplants
10 cloves garlic, crushed
½ teaspoon crushed black peppercorns
½ teaspoon red chili pepper flakes
1 teaspoon dried oregano
2 tablespoons pickling salt
3 cups water

1. Peel the eggplants and then thinly slice them. Pack them into a pint jar, layering them together with the garlic, peppercorns, chili pepper flakes, and oregano. In a small bowl, mix the salt and water, stirring until the salt is dissolved. Pour the brine over the eggplant. Use a small weight to hold the eggplant down under the brine. Loosely cap the jar with a nonreactive lid and leave the jar in a room temperature location.

2. After 7 days, remove the weight, cap the jar with a nonreactive lid, and transfer it to the refrigerator where the eggplant will keep for at least 1 month.

LACTO-FERMENTED KOHLRABI PICKLES

MAKES 1 QUART

Kohlrabi is often fermented shredded in the same way as cabbage or turnips. For this recipe, however, the kohlrabi is cut into spears to make pickles. Crisp and mild, kohlrabi so successfully soaks up the flavors of dill, peppercorns, and garlic that you'll be rushing back to the market to make more.

PREP TIME: 10 minutes
FERMENTATION TIME: 5 to 10 days

3 to 4 small kohlrabi bulbs, peeled
4 cloves garlic, crushed
3 dill heads
½ teaspoon crushed black peppercorns
2 dried chile peppers (optional)
1½ tablespoons pickling salt
3 cups water

1. Cut the kohlrabi into ½-inch-thick strips and transfer them to a quart jar, snugly layering them in with the garlic, dill heads, peppercorns, and chile peppers, if using. Mix the salt and water together until the salt is dissolved, and pour this brine over the kohlrabi. If needed, weigh the kohlrabi down so that it is submerged in the brine, and cap the jar loosely with a nonreactive lid. Place the jar in a room temperature location.

2. After 5 days, check the kohlrabi for taste. If they are to your liking, they are done. If they are not yet to your taste, reapply the weight and return them to the counter to ferment for up to 10 days total.

3. When fermentation is complete, remove the weight, cap the jar with a nonreactive lid, and transfer the jar to the refrigerator where the kohlrabi will keep for more than 1 month.

A CLOSER LOOK

Kohlrabi can grow rather large; however, they are the most sweet when they are small, around the size of a tennis ball. When shopping for kohlrabi, look for those with a firm, smooth skin that shows no signs of cracking, and vibrant fresh leaves.

LACTO-FERMENTED CELERY

MAKES 1 QUART

In American cuisine, celery is widely overlooked, used almost entirely as a flavoring agent instead of a vegetable on its own. Switch this up by fermenting and serving this simple pickle as a side. Look for fresh celery in season throughout the summer, as it is much sweeter than many supermarket varieties.

PREP TIME: 10 minutes
FERMENTATION TIME: 5 to 7 days

1 small to medium-size bunch of celery, thickly sliced

½ onion, peeled and sliced

4 cloves garlic, crushed

½ teaspoon red chili pepper flakes

1½ tablespoons pickling salt

2 cups water

1. Pack the celery in a quart jar, layering with the onion, garlic, and red chili pepper flakes. In a small bowl, mix the salt and water and pour this brine over the celery. Use a weight to keep the celery submerged, and cap the jar loosely using a nonreactive lid. Leave the jar in a room temperature location.

2. After 5 days, check the celery for taste. If it is to your liking, it is done. If you're not yet satisfied, reapply the weight and return the jar to the counter to ferment for up to 7 days total.

3. When fermentation is complete, remove the weight, cap the jar with a nonreactive lid, and transfer it to the refrigerator where the celery will keep for at least 1 month.

6

FRUIT PICKLES

Fruit may not be the first thing that comes to mind when you think of pickling. However, don't let that dissuade you from trying these complexly flavored pickles. Spanning the range of sweet to sour to spicy, there is definitely a fruit pickle to suit everyone's tastes.

Look for firm fruits when using them for pickling, especially for recipes that will be water-bath canned, as well-ripened fruits will often lose too much of their structure after pickling, This chapter contains a mix of fresh and fermented pickles, so be sure to check which process you'll be doing before you begin, to be sure you have all the necessary equipment ready to go.

PICKLED APPLES

MAKES 1 PINT

This quick and easy refrigerator pickle makes use of those couple extra apples you have lying around the kitchen. While any variety of apple can work—including crab apples—apples with red skin will lend a nice hue to the finished pickles.

PREP TIME: 15 minutes
COOK TIME: 6 minutes
CURING TIME: 8 hours

¾ pound apples
1 cup apple cider vinegar
½ cup water
¾ cup sugar
1 (4-inch) cinnamon stick, broken
1 teaspoon allspice berries
½ teaspoon black peppercorns
3 whole cloves

1. Halve and core the apples and then thinly slice.

2. In a nonreactive pot, combine the remaining ingredients and bring to a boil. Reduce the heat, stirring until the sugar dissolves.

3. Add the apples and return the brine to a boil. Reduce the heat, cover, and simmer the apples for 3 minutes.

4. Transfer the apples to a jar or bowl and set on the counter until they come to room temperature. Cover the apples with a nonreactive lid and store them refrigerated for at least 8 hours. Store them for up to 1 month.

A CLOSER LOOK

There is often an abundance of apples available in the fall, but not all apples are created equally, especially when it comes to cooking. Look for Gala, Granny Smith, Pink Lady, Braeburn, or Fuji apples. All are good choices that hold up well to heat processing.

LACTO-FERMENTED SPICED APPLES

MAKES 1 QUART

Lacto-fermented apples are surprisingly just as pleasing as quick-pickled ones, though notably more soured than sweet. Using just salt, lemon juice, cinnamon, and honey, apples are transformed into this simple sweet and sour ferment. Eat them as a snack, or serve them with meats for a tasty side dish.

PREP TIME: 20 minutes
FERMENTATION TIME: 5 to 7 days
CURING TIME: 1 week

1 tablespoon honey
1 tablespoon pickling salt
1 (4-inch) cinnamon stick, broken
4 cups water
Juice of 1 lemon
Zest of 1 lemon
1 pound sweet apples

1. In a nonreactive pot, combine the honey, salt, cinnamon, water, lemon juice, and lemon zest. Heat until the salt is dissolved then promptly turn off the heat. Let the mixture cool to room temperature.

2. Halve and core the apples; then thinly slice the halves and pack them into a quart jar.

3. Pour the cooled brine over the apples, pressing the apples down to ensure they are below the brine. Use a weight, or add the remaining brine to a food-safe, zippered plastic bag and insert this into the neck of the bottle to hold the apples below the brine.

4. Allow the apples to sit at room temperature for 5 to 7 days until fermentation slows down. At this point remove the weight, affix a nonreactive lid, and refrigerate the pickled apples for at least 1 week before eating. Refrigerated, the apples will keep for 1 month.

PICKLED PEARS

MAKES 3 PINTS

Pears are surprisingly uplifting in the dead of winter, and this pickled variety does not disappoint. If you can find them, use a small variety and leave the pears whole for a stunning presentation or, if need be, halve them to fit in the jars. Be sure to treat the pears for darkening immediately after you cut them to prevent discoloration (see next page). Seckel, Bartlett, and Comice pears are the best choices for pickling.

PREP TIME: 15 minutes
PROCESSING TIME: 10 minutes
CURING TIME: 1 week

2 pounds pears

1½ cups sugar

1½ cups water

1½ cups white vinegar

1 teaspoon cloves

3 cinnamon sticks

1 (1-inch) piece of ginger, peeled and
   thinly sliced

1. Halve and core the pears or, if desired, leave whole. Treat for browning (see next page), and pack into the jars.

2. In a nonreactive pot, combine the sugar, water, and vinegar. Bring to a boil.

3. Divide the cloves, cinnamon sticks, and ginger between the jars. Pour the hot brine over the pears, use a nonreactive utensil to remove air bubbles, and leave ½ inch of headspace. Wipe the rims and cap the jars using two-piece canning lids.

4. Process in a boiling-water bath for 10 minutes. Store the jars in a cool, dark, and dry location for at least 1 week before eating.

PAIR WITH

Pears work wonderfully with cheeses such as feta and goat cheese. Serve these pickled pears atop a salad of greens, and you have a fantastic starter loaded with a world of flavor.

HOW TO PREVENT DISCOLORATION IN FRUITS

When working with pears, apples, peaches, and other fruits that are prone to discoloration, it is a good idea to treat them before processing to prevent browning. There are several different ways to do this. Some of the easiest, cheapest, and best include:

- **ASCORBIC ACID:** Otherwise known as vitamin C, ascorbic acid prevents the oxidation that causes browning in fruits. It can be found in the canning department of many large stores, and also in the supplement department in powdered form. To use, mix 1 teaspoon per 2 cups of water, and soak the fruit in this solution for 10 minutes immediately after cutting.

- **LEMON JUICE:** Lemon juice works in the same way as ascorbic acid, and is widely available bottled at any grocery store. Add 2 tablespoons to 2 cups of water, and soak the cut fruit for 10 minutes immediately after cutting.

- **COMMERCIAL FRUIT TREATMENT:** There are a couple of products sold commercially that are especially designed to treat fruit for discoloration before canning. The most widely available is Fruit Fresh. This product contains citric acid, the same type of acid found in lemons and limes. To use, follow directions on the packaging.

6

FRUIT PICKLES

PICKLED PEACHES

In theory and practice, pickled peaches can be canned, but because of the extended processing time needed to ensure safety, they end up fairly mushy. Therefore, this recipe is not meant for canning. Instead, it produces a still-firm peach that holds up quite well. Try Pickled Peaches and Yogurt (page 146) for a delicious snack.

PREP TIME: 40 minutes
COOK TIME: 25 minutes
CURING TIME: 1 day

2 teaspoons mixed pickling spice

¼ teaspoon red chili pepper flakes

1 cinnamon stick

4 cups water

2 cups white vinegar

1½ cups sugar

1½ teaspoons pickling salt

2 pounds peaches, peeled, quartered, pitted

1. In a nonreactive pot, combine the mixed pickling spice, red chili pepper flakes, cinnamon, water, vinegar, sugar, and salt. Bring to a boil, stirring to dissolve the sugar. Lower the heat to simmer.

2. Add the peaches and continue to simmer until the peaches are just tender, about 20 minutes.

3. Transfer the peaches to a jar, covering with the pickling liquid. Cool to room temperature and then refrigerate for 1 day before eating.

A CLOSER LOOK

To remove peach skin, as well as other thick-skinned fruits, cut an "X" in the skin with a paring knife. Blanch the peaches briefly, about 30 seconds, in boiling water, and immediately transfer them to an ice-cold bath. The skins should slip off easily after this. If they don't, blanch them a little longer and try again.

PICKLED BLUEBERRIES

MAKES 1 PINT

Similar to a blueberry relish or ketchup, this pickle is unique in that it's made with whole blueberries. Somewhat akin to cranberry relish, this pairs well with dinner, especially ham and poultry. Or if you like, spoon it over a bowl of ice cream for a sweet and sour combination that is a treat for the taste buds.

PREP TIME: 20 minutes, plus 12 hours resting time
COOK TIME: 12 minutes
CURING TIME: 48 hours

3½ cups blueberries
1 cup red wine vinegar
1 cinnamon stick, broken
3 whole cloves
2 whole star anise
2 whole cardamom pods
1 (1-inch) piece of ginger, peeled and thinly sliced
½ cup sugar

1. Wash and pick through the blueberries, removing any that are mushy or bruised.

2. Pour the vinegar in a nonreactive pot. Create a spice bag using a piece of cheesecloth, and add to it the cinnamon stick, cloves, star anise, cardamom, and ginger. Simmer over low heat, covered, for 5 minutes.

3. Gently add the blueberries to the pot and cook until just heated through. Shake the pot to mix the berries instead of stirring, to keep the berries whole.

4. Remove the pot from the heat, cover it, and let it sit for 12 hours at room temperature.

5. The following day, using a slotted spoon, remove the berries from the liquid and transfer to a sterile pint jar.

6. Add the sugar to the spiced vinegar. Bring the liquid to a boil, stirring to dissolve the sugar. Boil the syrup until it just begins to thicken, about 3 to 4 minutes. Pour the hot liquid over the berries and seal the jar using a two-piece lid.

7. Refrigerate the berries for at least 48 hours before eating.

TRY INSTEAD

For a similar pickle, you can also make this recipe using blackberries. Just be sure to pick through the berries well to ensure they are firm before using.

MINTY PICKLED STRAWBERRIES

Pickling strawberries intensifies their flavor and gives them an infused edge that pairs especially well with other foods. Try these on toasted bread with goat cheese, or add them to a green salad. Either way, they liven up a plate and bring a welcome dose of summer to any meal.

PREP TIME: 20 minutes
COOK TIME: 5 minutes
CURING TIME: 2 days

2 pints strawberries

10 to 12 fresh mint leaves

¾ cup balsamic vinegar

¼ cup rice vinegar

½ cup water

½ cup sugar

2 whole star anise

2 whole cloves

1 cinnamon stick, broken

1 (1-inch) piece of ginger, peeled and sliced

1. Wash and hull the strawberries. Halve them if desired. Pack the strawberries and mint leaves into sterile jars.

2. In a nonreactive pot, combine the vinegars, water, sugar, star anise, cloves, cinnamon, and ginger. Bring to a boil, then turn off the heat. Remove the star anise from the spiced vinegar and pour the liquid over the strawberries. Cap the jar with a nonreactive lid.

3. Refrigerate the strawberries for at least 2 days before serving.

SWEET PICKLED CHERRIES

MAKES 1 PINT

Whether you have access to sweet or sour cherries, you can make this simple recipe that is bold in both its sweetness and cherry flavor. Serve the cherries on a salad, or alongside smoked meats to enjoy this taste of summer at its finest.

PREP TIME: 10 minutes, plus 3 days resting time
COOK TIME: 10 minutes
CURING TIME: 1 month

1 pound sweet or sour cherries, stemmed and pitted

1½ cups white vinegar

¾ cup sugar

Seeds of 1 cardamom pod

1 cinnamon stick

1. Place the cherries in a nonreactive bowl and cover them with the vinegar. Cover the bowl and let the cherries stand at room temperature for 3 days.

2. Strain the vinegar into a nonreactive pot. Add the sugar, cardamom seeds, and cinnamon stick. Bring the liquid to a boil, then turn it down and simmer for 10 minutes.

3. Pour the hot liquid over the cherries, and then use a nonreactive lid to tightly cap the jar. Store the jars in a cool, dark, and dry location for at least 1 month before eating.

A CLOSER LOOK

Cherries are one of the most pesticide-contaminated fruits, so choosing organic cherries is a good idea, especially for children and pregnant women. Seeking out an organic supplier is advisable if you eat cherries regularly.

BRINED CHERRIES

Difficult to define in flavor, these brined cherries are best served cold with accompanying cheeses and other antipasto offerings. The cherries should sink so there is no need to weight them, but if you find that some float to the top, hold them down with a small weight. These cherries are brined with their pits so you'll need a smaller quantity than is used for the Sweet Pickled Cherries.

PREP TIME: 30 minutes
COOK TIME: none
CURING TIME: 1 week

¾ pound cherries
2 hot chile peppers, slit lengthwise
2 garlic cloves, crushed
¼ teaspoon black peppercorns
1 bay leaf
1 tablespoon pickling salt
1½ cups water

1. Place the cherries, chile peppers, garlic, peppercorns, and bay leaf in a pint jar.

2. In a bowl, dissolve the salt in the water and pour this brine over the cherries. Cap the jar loosely with a nonreactive lid and leave at room temperature for 1 week.

3. Transfer to the refrigerator where they will keep for 1 month.

PICKLED PLUMS

Pickled plums, like many other pickled fruits, work both as condiments and as a simple dessert when paired with ice cream or yogurt. Because plums are lower in acid than many other fruits, the vinegar enhances the flavor so much you may wonder why you have never tried them before. Choose firm plums to ensure the fruits are still intact after cooking.

PREP TIME: 10 minutes
COOK TIME: 7 minutes
CURING TIME: 1 month

2 pounds Italian plums

1½ cups red wine vinegar

½ cup sugar

1 cinnamon stick, broken in half

4 whole cloves

1 teaspoon cardamom seeds

1 (2-inch) piece of ginger, peeled and thinly sliced

1. Use a skewer to poke each plum three times. In a nonreactive pot, combine the vinegar and sugar. Bring to a boil, stirring to dissolve the sugar. Add the plums to the pot and lower the heat to simmer. Continue to cook for a few minutes until the plums are heated through.

2. While the plums are cooking, divide the cinnamon stick, cloves, cardamom seeds, and ginger between two sterile quart jars.

3. Transfer the plums to the jars and ladle in the syrup to cover them. Cap the jars using nonreactive lids and store the plums in a cool, dark, and dry location for 1 month before opening. Once opened, refrigerate.

TRY INSTEAD

If you are unable to find Italian plums, you can substitute other dark varieties here instead. However, be sure to pick plums that are slightly underripe, rather than fully ripe ones more appropriate for fresh eating.

LACTO-FERMENTED PLUMS

MAKES 1 QUART

Lacto-fermented plums have a distinctly different taste than the pickled variety, employing only salt to develop their soured flavor. Slice these plums thinly and serve with cheeses, cold meats, and firm breads for a light meal, or add them to a green salad or coleslaw for some added zip.

PREP TIME: 30 minutes
FERMENTATION TIME: 3 days
CURING TIME: 1 week

1 pound firm plums
2 cups water
1 tablespoon pickling salt

1. Using a skewer, poke the plums three times each and place them in a sterile quart jar.

2. In a bowl, mix the water and salt until the salt is dissolved. Pour this brine over the plums and cap the jar loosely with a nonreactive lid.

3. Leave the jar at room temperature for 3 days. Transfer it to the refrigerator and leave the plums for at least 1 additional week before eating. Store the plums for up to 3 months.

SPICED WATERMELON PICKLES

MAKES 3 PINTS

After trying this pickle, you may never throw away your watermelon rinds again. While it may take a bit of work to prepare the rind, it is well worth it when you taste this classic Southern pickle. For this pickle you use the white part of watermelon rind. After eating the pink flesh, cut away any remaining pink portions as well as the green outer skin, leaving just the white rind, which should be about ¼- to ½-inch thick.

PREP TIME: 20 minutes, plus 36 hours resting
COOK TIME: 25 minutes
PROCESSING TIME: 10 minutes

¼ cup pickling salt
6 cups prepared watermelon rind
1½ cups white vinegar
1½ cups water
2 cups sugar
2 cinnamon sticks
½ teaspoon whole cloves
½ teaspoon allspice

1. In a nonreactive bowl, add 4 cups of water and the pickling salt, stirring to combine. Add the watermelon rind and use a small plate to hold the pieces down in the brine. Leave at room temperature overnight.

2. The following day, drain the watermelon rind. Fill the bowl with water again, and drain again.

3. In a nonreactive pot, combine the remaining ingredients and bring them to a boil. Turn down the heat and simmer for 10 minutes. Add the watermelon rind pieces and turn off the heat. Leave the syrup in the pot for up to 24 hours.

4. Bring the mixture back to a boil and simmer the rinds for 5 to 10 minutes, until they become translucent. Remove the pot from the heat.

5. Pack the watermelon rinds and the syrup into the jars. Cap the jars using two-piece canning lids. Process in a boiling-water bath for 10 minutes. Store the jars in a cool, dark, and dry location.

LACTO-FERMENTED WATERMELON PICKLES

MAKES 1 QUART

If you like the taste of watermelon rind pickles, but want to add some probiotic punch to your daily diet, here is a fun way to do it. These pickles don't have any added sugar, making them more sour than the Spiced Watermelon Pickles. However that doesn't mean that they are any less delicious. This is a basic fermentation recipe, so feel free to include any additional spices to give it your personal twist. See the Spiced Watermelon Pickles (page 93) for how to prepare the rind.

PREP TIME: 15 minutes
COOK TIME: none
FERMENTATION TIME: 5 to 7 days

4 cups prepared watermelon rind
1 quart water
2 tablespoons pickling salt

1. Pack the watermelon rind into a quart jar.

2. Mix the water and pickling salt in a bowl until the salt is dissolved. Pour this solution over the watermelon rinds. Use a nonreactive utensil to check for air bubbles and if necessary, use a small weight to hold the watermelon rinds below the surface. Loosely cap the jar using a nonreactive lid.

3. Leave the jar at room temperature for 5 to 7 days, or until an appetizing flavor and texture has been produced. Close the jar tightly and transfer it to the refrigerator, where the flavor will continue to develop over time.

PICKLED FIGS

MAKES 4 PINTS

Pickled figs are not a common fruit pickle, but that says nothing about how delicious they actually are. If you have access to a fig tree, snag a couple pounds for this rewarding project, or source figs at a farmers' market in the summer when they are at their peak.

PREP TIME: 30 minutes
COOK TIME: 25 minutes
PROCESSING TIME: 15 minutes

2 cups sugar

4 cups water

1 cinnamon stick

1 teaspoon whole cloves

1 teaspoon whole allspice

2½ pounds firm, but ripe figs

1½ cups apple cider vinegar

1. In a nonreactive pot, combine the sugar, water, cinnamon, cloves, and allspice. Bring to a boil, stirring to dissolve the sugar. Lower the heat to simmer and carefully add the figs. Stir the figs gently as they simmer for about 20 minutes until they are tender. Add the vinegar and continue to cook until the liquid begins simmering again.

2. Ladle the figs into pint jars and cover with the syrup, leaving ½ inch of headspace.

3. Process in a boiling-water bath for 15 minutes. Store the jars in a cool, dry, dark location.

A CLOSER LOOK

Figs are loaded with fiber and a great addition to the diet. When looking for figs for pickling, be sure to select ones that are firm but ripe without blemishes. In most regions of the country, this is not a problem, as they are most often picked when underripe to allow for transport.

FRUIT PICKLES

PICKLED KUMQUATS

Kumquats are only available for a short time in the winter, but when you can find them, this is definitely a sweet-and-sour pickle worth trying. Once you have finished with the bite-sized morsels, don't dump out the vinegar—use it for dressings and to season other dishes.

PREP TIME: 20 minutes
COOK TIME: 10 minutes
PROCESSING TIME: 10 minutes

1 ½ pounds kumquats
2 cups white vinegar
½ cup sugar
1 teaspoon pickling salt
2 whole star anise
4 cardamom pods
½ teaspoon black peppercorns
1 (1-inch) piece of ginger, peeled and sliced

1. Wash the kumquats and remove any that are bruised. Remove the stem end with a sharp knife and cut each piece in half. Remove any seeds present with the tip of the knife.

2. Add the kumquats to a nonreactive pan. Cover with water, bring to a boil, turn off the heat, and let the kumquats sit for about 15 minutes. Drain in a colander.

3. Combine the vinegar, sugar, and salt in the pan. Make a spice bag using a small piece of cheesecloth and kitchen twine. Add all the remaining ingredients to the bag and lower it into the pot. Bring the ingredients to a boil and lower the heat to simmer the syrup for 2 minutes. Add the kumquats back to the syrup and continue to simmer for an additional 2 minutes.

4. Ladle the kumquats and syrup into the prepared jars and cap the jars with two-piece canning lids.

5. Process the jars in a boiling-water bath for 10 minutes.

6. Store the jars in a cool, dry, dark location.

FRUIT PICKLES

6

PICKLED LEMONS

Unlike many other pickled lemon recipes, this one has added sugar to give it the benefit of sweetness, making it an ideal starting point for someone new to this delicacy. Commonly served alongside meals in India and Morocco, pickled lemon is a delicious condiment that complements both meat and vegetable dishes.

PREP TIME: 10 minutes
COOK TIME: 12 minutes
CURING TIME: 1 week, plus 1 month

2 small lemons
1 teaspoon cumin seeds
1 teaspoon black peppercorns
1 tablespoon pickling salt
3 tablespoons lemon juice
1 cup brown sugar

1. Cut the lemons in half lengthwise and then thinly slice them. In a spice grinder or with a mortar and pestle, grind the cumin and peppercorns. Mix the spices together with the pickling salt. In a half-pint jar, layer the lemon slices with the salt-spice mixture, packing them down as you go. Cover the lemons with the lemon juice. Place the jar in a warm location and let it sit for at least 7 days.

2. Pour the juice from the jar into a nonreactive pan, pressing as you do to extract more juice from the lemons. Add the sugar and slowly bring the mixture to a simmer, stirring to dissolve the sugar. Add the lemons and simmer for an additional 10 minutes.

3. Pack the lemons and juices back into a half-pint jar, cap the jar tightly, and leave the jar at room temperature for 1 month. Transfer the jar to the refrigerator, where it will keep for several months.

A CLOSER LOOK

When using entire lemons, select organic lemons, as commercial lemons are waxed, dyed, and have considerable pesticide and fungicide residues.

FRUIT PICKLES

6

7

KIMCHI, TSUKEMONO, AND OTHER PICKLES OF THE EAST

Kimchi, a fermented Korean pickle, and tsukemono, a wide variety of fragrantly pickled foods hailing from Japan, are in a league of their own. Used as a garnish, snack, or side dish, these simple pickles represent a wide range of styles, burst with individuality, and are served with nearly every traditional meal in their respective place of origin. Whether fermented, salt-cured, or miso-cured, these pickles shine with crunch and are a great addition to your kitchen.

CABBAGE KIMCHI

MAKES 1 QUART

Kimchi is the national treasure of Korea, and this simple, basic cabbage kimchi is the star of the show. Use Chinese cabbage when making kimchi, as it is much more tender than European varieties of cabbage. You can adjust the heat level here to suit your preference, and, if desired, add in some complementary elements such as sliced daikon or turnip.

PREP TIME: 10 minutes, plus 12 hours resting time
FERMENTATION TIME: 3 to 6 days

2 tablespoons, plus ¾ teaspoon
    pickling salt, divided
4 cups water
1½ pounds Chinese cabbage, cut into
    1-inch squares
5 scallions, cut into 1-inch lengths, then slivered
1 tablespoon minced ginger
1½ tablespoons Korean ground dried hot pepper
¾ teaspoon sugar

1. In a nonreactive bowl, dissolve 2 tablespoons of salt in the water. Place the cabbage in the water and weigh them down using a plate. Leave the bowl, covered with a kitchen towel, at room temperature for 12 hours.

2. Strain the cabbage, reserving the brine. Transfer the cabbage to another bowl and mix together with all the remaining ingredients, including the remaining ¾ teaspoon of salt.

3. Pack the cabbage mixture into a quart jar. Cover it with the reserved brine until the cabbage is submerged. Use a small weight to hold the cabbage down, or pour the remaining brine into a food-safe zippered plastic bag and press this into the mouth of the jar to weight down the cabbage.

4. Place the jar in a location that stays around 68°F, and leave it to ferment for 3 to 6 days, or until soured to your liking.

5. Remove the weight and close the jar tightly with a nonreactive lid. Store refrigerated, where it will keep for several months.

A CLOSER LOOK

If you don't have access to a market that carries Korean hot pepper, that's okay. Simply use another mild hot pepper powder such as New Mexican ground hot peppers, or Mexican pepper blends.

CABBAGE, CARROT, CUCUMBER, AND BROCCOLI KIMCHI

MAKES 1½ QUARTS

Cabbage is a given, but you may never have even considered adding carrot, cucumber, and broccoli to your kimchi. The fact is, these all work exceptionally well for providing added depth to the spice and sourness of kimchi. Because broccoli is so tough, it is important to cut it into small pieces, especially its fibrous stems, to enjoy eating it in this lightly fermented state.

PREP TIME: 15 minutes, plus 12 hours resting time
FERMENTATION TIME: 3 to 6 days

3 tablespoons, plus 1 teaspoon pickling salt, divided

6 cups water

1 pound Chinese cabbage, cut into 1-inch squares

2 cucumbers, peeled and julienned

3 carrots, peeled and julienned

2 small heads broccoli, divided into florets, and the stems cut into ¼-inch rounds

6 scallions, cut into rounds

1 tablespoon minced ginger

2 tablespoons Korean ground dried hot pepper

1 teaspoon sugar

1. In a nonreactive bowl, dissolve 3 tablespoons of salt in the water. Place the cabbage and cucumbers in the water and weigh them down using a plate. Leave the bowl, covered with a kitchen towel, at room temperature for 12 hours.

2. Strain the cabbage and cucumbers, reserving the brine. Transfer the mixture to another bowl and mix it together with all the remaining ingredients, including the remaining 1 teaspoon of salt.

3. Pack the vegetable mixture into a 2-quart jar. Cover with the reserved brine, until the cabbage is submerged. Use a small weight to hold the cabbage down, or pour the remaining brine into a food-safe zippered plastic bag, and press this into the mouth of the jar to weigh down the cabbage.

4. Place the jar in a location that stays around 68°F, and leave it to ferment for 3 to 6 days, or until soured to your liking.

5. Remove the weight and close the jar tightly with a nonreactive lid. Store it refrigerated, where it will keep for several months.

KALE AND CARROT KIMCHI

MAKES 1 QUART

Kale is a nutritional beast, and here it is combined with just the right amount of Korean hot pepper powder to create a fire-hot quick kimchi that skips the fermentation step. Blanching the kale makes it tender, while a combination of ginger, scallions, and sugar seasons it just the right amount, creating a perfect side dish for an Asian-inspired meal.

PREP TIME: 25 minutes
CURING TIME: 4 hours

4 pounds kale, cleaned, stalks removed, and cut into 2-inch squares

1 tablespoon kosher salt

¾ cup water

¼ cup sugar

2 tablespoons minced garlic

1½ tablespoons minced ginger

4 scallions, cut into 2-inch lengths, then julienned

1 carrot, peeled and cut into 2-inch lengths, then julienned

2 tablespoons Korean ground dried hot pepper

¼ cup cut strips of Asian pear

1. Prepare an ice bath, and bring a large pot of water to a boil. Submerge the kale into the boiling water and blanch for 3 minutes. Promptly remove the kale and transfer it to the ice bath. Once cool, drain the water and press the kale with your hands to remove as much water as possible. Toss the kale with the salt and set aside.

2. In a large bowl, combine the water with the sugar, and stir to dissolve. Add the garlic, ginger, scallions, carrot, and hot pepper powder. Mix to combine. Add the kale and Asian pear and stir until mixed well.

3. Pack tightly into a quart jar, pressing firmly as you go. Close the jar with a nonreactive lid and refrigerate for at least 4 hours before serving. Refrigerated, it will keep for around 7 days.

TRY INSTEAD

Asian pears have a mildly sweet flavor. If you don't have access to Asian pears, substitute a tart apple, which most closely resembles the flavor of this fruit.

CUCUMBER KIMCHI

MAKES 2 CUPS

Cucumber kimchi made in this way is a Japanese quick-version of the traditionally fermented side dish. Try this out when you're looking for the taste of kimchi but don't want to wait for fermentation to take place. Place it in the refrigerator when it is complete, and serve it cold after just a couple hours of rest. Use Japanese cucumbers for the best results. You can usually find them at your grocer. They are longer and thinner than their American counterpart and have very few seeds.

In a nonreactive bowl, mix the cucumbers, apple, radishes, ginger, and lemon rind. Add the hot pepper powder, salt, sugar, and vinegar. Pour the water over the kimchi. Cover the bowl and refrigerate for 2 hours before serving.

TRY INSTEAD

If you like, swap the salt out for 1 teaspoon of soy sauce. This adds a different complexity to the kimchi. Though soy sauce is not a traditional flavoring in kimchi, it plays well off the cucumbers and creates a quick kimchi that is equally delicious.

PREP TIME: 10 minutes
CURING TIME: 2 hours

3 Japanese cucumbers, thinly sliced

1 small, tart apple, cored and thinly sliced

6 radishes, sliced

1 (1-inch) piece of ginger, peeled and sliced

½ lemon rind, grated on microplane grater

1 teaspoon Korean dried hot pepper powder

½ teaspoon salt

1½ teaspoons sugar

1 tablespoon rice vinegar

¾ cup water

PICKLED GINGER

MAKES 1 CUP

This is the type of pickled ginger that is served with sushi. It is typically made with young ginger, which becomes available in the early summer at farmers' markets. Whether you have access to young ginger or not, you can make this by peeling the ginger before using, and slicing it super thin.

PREP TIME: 10 minutes
COOK TIME: 5 minutes
CURING TIME: 2 to 3 days

2 cups water
1 teaspoon, plus ½ teaspoon salt, divided
3 ounces ginger, peeled and thinly sliced
½ cup rice vinegar
2 tablespoons sugar

1. In a pot, mix the water and 1 teaspoon of salt. Bring the liquid to a boil and add the ginger to the pot. Cook for 30 seconds and drain the water.

2. Pack the ginger into a sterilized jar.

3. In a nonreactive pot, mix the vinegar, sugar, and the remaining ½ teaspoon of salt. Bring this liquid to a boil, remove it from the heat, and allow it to come to room temperature.

4. Pour the cooled liquid over the ginger, and store refrigerated. It's best to eat after 2 to 3 days, but will keep indefinitely.

TRY INSTEAD

If you want to speed up the process, cool the brine by placing the bottom of the pot in a cold water bath to cool it to room temperature. Because this recipe uses a small amount of liquid, this should only take a couple minutes to cool down when using this method.

GARLIC IN SOY SAUCE

MAKES 2 CUPS

This pickle is made using young garlic, which has paper-thin skin that, for the most part, can be left intact. Look for young garlic at the beginning of the summer, when harvest begins to take place. After 2 months of curing, the garlic odor will be drastically diminished, and you are left with a delicious, crisp garlic pickle that has just the perfect amount of sweet and savory.

PREP TIME: 10 minutes
CURING TIME: 2 months

5 to 6 whole garlic heads
1 cup rice vinegar
⅔ cup soy sauce
1 tablespoon sugar

1. Peel only the outermost layer of skin from the garlic heads. Trim away the stems to allow you to pack the garlic tightly.

2. Pack the garlic into a sterile pint jar. Cover with the vinegar, close the jar with a nonreactive lid, and leave at room temperature for 2 weeks.

3. Strain the vinegar off the garlic, reserving the vinegar. Measure ⅓ cup of the reserved vinegar, and mix it with the soy sauce and sugar until the sugar is dissolved. Pour this mixture over the garlic, cover with a nonreactive lid, and store the garlic refrigerated for at least 1½ months before eating. To serve, cut the garlic heads diagonally through the head and serve each half whole.

A CLOSER LOOK

For pickles that will be refrigerated for a long time, or those prone to spoilage, a sterilized jar is called for to prevent the growth of mold, which can occur even when the pickle is refrigerated. To sterilize jars, simply boil them for 10 minutes before using.

MISO GARLIC

MAKES 2 CUPS

Miso, a fermented soybean paste, is a perfect pickling medium, especially for ever-so-pungent garlic. If the thought of eating raw garlic does not appeal to you, consider trying this; you may be surprised. After about a week, the intense flavor of the garlic mellows, producing a tasty meal accompaniment. Mix the pickles into cooked rice for a fragrant dish, or roast them in sesame oil until browned for an excellent complement to meat.

PREP TIME: 10 minutes
COOK TIME: 5 minutes
CURING TIME: 1 week

8 ounces peeled garlic cloves
8 ounces miso
3 tablespoons mirin

1. Fill a small pot with water and bring it to a boil. Add the garlic and cook for 2 minutes. Drain. Using a clean kitchen towel, pat the cloves entirely dry.

2. Mix the miso and mirin in a small bowl. Add about half of this mixture to the bottom of a pint jar. Place the garlic cloves into the jar and cover them with the remaining miso paste mixture, pressing it down so that the cloves are well covered.

3. Cover the jar using a nonreactive lid, and refrigerate for at least 1 week before eating.

A CLOSER LOOK

There are several types of miso paste available, the most common being red and white miso. This pickle is typically made using red miso, which is stronger in flavor. However, it is perfectly fine to experiment with different types of miso paste. Try making these with your favorite variety and see what you think.

DAIKON IN SOY SAUCE

MAKES 1½ CUPS

If you don't want to wait for takuan (pickled daikon), here is a quick pickle you can eat in about an hour. Daikon, a thick white radish, helps with digestion, and you will have no problem enjoying plenty of it in this salty, flavorful brine.

PREP TIME: 15 minutes, plus 1 hour resting time
CURING TIME: 1 to 2 hours

1 pound daikon peeled, cut lengthwise, and cut into half moons
1 teaspoon pickling salt
½ lemon
3 tablespoons soy sauce
1 tablespoon mirin
1-inch piece kombu, cut into small pieces

1. Sprinkle the daikon with the salt, toss in a bowl, and allow to sit for 1 hour. Drain off any water.

2. Remove the rind from the lemon and dice the rind finely. In a nonreactive bowl, mix the soy sauce and mirin. Add the lemon rind, kombu, and daikon and mix well.

3. Cover the bowl with a small plate and weigh down the plate using a large stone or jar filled with water. Halfway through the curing time, mix the seasoned daikon and weigh it down again. Serve after 1 or 2 hours.

A CLOSER LOOK

Kombu, used in Japanese cuisine to make savory stocks, is a type of seaweed. It is used both as a flavoring agent and served in salads and other fresh preparations. It is high in vitamins A and C, as well as iodine, calcium, and potassium. It is best to cut kombu with kitchen shears.

SPICY PICKLED DAIKON

MAKES 1½ CUPS

This quick pickle makes a nice, spicy side, or add it to a stir-fry to heat things up a bit. While overnight refrigeration adds to the intensity of the flavors, this simple pickle can be eaten as soon as 2 hours after preparation.

PREP TIME: 15 minutes, plus 30 minutes
    resting time
CURING TIME: 2 hours

1 pound daikon, peeled and cut into matchsticks
1 teaspoon salt
3 cloves garlic, minced
2 scallions, finely sliced
1 teaspoon toasted sesame seeds
1 tablespoon rice vinegar
½ teaspoon red chili pepper flakes
1 teaspoon sugar

1. Toss the daikon with the salt in a bowl and let sit for about 30 minutes. Drain the daikon and squeeze out any additional water using your hands.

2. Add the remaining ingredients and mix well. Pack the mixture into a pint jar and store for at least 2 hours before serving.

A CLOSER LOOK

To toast sesame seeds, place them in a dry skillet over medium-high heat. Cook them for 3 to 5 minutes, stirring frequently, until they become lightly browned. To prevent them from burning, remove them to a cool plate as soon as their color starts to change.

TAKUAN (PICKLED DAIKON)

MAKES 2 POUNDS

If you buy takuan, a type of pickled daikon, at the store, it is most likely dyed with chemicals to give it its bright yellow coloring. By pickling the daikon at home, you can achieve the same flavor and crunch without all the chemicals. It will take at least a month to achieve a good flavor, and even longer to develop flavors that are really complex, but this classic Japanese pickle is worth the wait. You will need a 1-gallon pickling crock or another similarly sized container made of wood or food-grade ceramic.

PREP TIME: 15 minutes, plus 2 to 3 weeks
   drying time
FERMENTATION TIME: 1 to 3 months

2 pounds daikon radish, preferably 2 or 3 thin and long ones

1/3 pound rice or wheat bran

4 tablespoons pickling salt

1/2 teaspoon brown sugar

2 dried chile peppers, finely diced

1 (2-inch) square kombu, cut into several smaller pieces

1. Rinse the daikon well, then hang outside in the sun, sheltered from rain, for 2 to 3 weeks. When the daikon are easily bendable, they are ready for pickling.

2. Using your hands, roll the daikon on a cutting board to further soften the radish.

3. In a bowl, mix the rice or wheat bran, salt, sugar, and chile peppers. Add one quarter of this mixture to the bottom of your pickling crock. Add half of the kombu to the crock if you have 2 radishes, one-third if you have 3 radishes. Layer the daikon into the crock, bending it so that it fits in the bottom of the crock. Cover the radish with a layer of the bran mixture, add half or one-third of the kombu, pack the next radish into the crock and then cover it with another portion of the bran mixture. If you have another radish, add it to the crock and use the remaining kombu and the bran mixture to cover the daikon.

4. Place a small plate into the crock to cover the bran mixture and cover the entire crock with a plastic bag. Place a heavy weight, around 4 to 6 pounds, on the plate to hold it down. Store the crock in a cool location.

5. After 5 days, remove the weight and inspect the crock. If the liquid has begun to rise, you can reduce the weight to 2 pounds. If not, continue with the heavier weight until the liquid rises.

6. After 1 month, remove a daikon, slice a piece, and taste it. If you like the flavor, remove the daikon and eat it now. If not, let it continue pickling for up to 2 more months.

A CLOSER LOOK

To infuse even more flavor into the daikon, try adding dried fruit peels to the pickling crock. Sun-dry the peels of apple, orange, lemon, or pear, and add them to the crock at the time of packing.

EGGPLANT PICKLED IN SOY SAUCE

Use small Japanese eggplants or another Asian variety for this recipe, not the globe eggplants found in many supermarkets. These slender eggplants are tender when raw and easily penetrated with this marinating mixture. One plant in the garden will produce an abundance of eggplants over the summer, or you can find them at Asian and specialty retailers.

PREP TIME: 5 minutes, plus 30 minutes resting time
CURING TIME: 2 hours

4 Japanese eggplants
1 (4-inch) square kombu, cut into small shreds
¾ cup soy sauce
1 tablespoon sake
½ teaspoon hot red chili pepper flakes

1. Halve the eggplants lengthwise. Using a sharp knife, make several small slits in the skin of the eggplant. Transfer the eggplants to a bowl and cover with cold water. Soak for 30 minutes. Drain the eggplants, cut them into 1-inch pieces, and return them to the bowl.

2. Add the remaining ingredients and stir to combine. Cover the jar with a nonreactive lid and leave it at room temperature for 2 hours. Shake the jar occasionally during this time.

3. Transfer the jar to the refrigerator and store in the refrigerator for up to 1 week.

QUICK-PICKLED CUCUMBERS

MAKES 2 CUPS

Meant to be eaten the morning following preparation, these pickles are delicious with any meal. While they pair exquisitely with Japanese meals, they can also be enjoyed alongside sandwiches and other Western fare. To serve, spoon a few pieces into an individual serving dish.

PREP TIME: 5 minutes
CURING TIME: 12 hours

4 Asian-style pickling cucumbers
1 (2-inch) square kombu, cut into small strips
4 tablespoons soy sauce
1 tablespoon mirin

1. Wash and dry the cucumbers and cut them into ½-inch-thick slices.

2. Rinse the kombu and place in the jar with the cucumbers.

3. In a small bowl, mix the soy sauce and mirin. Pour this mixture over the cucumbers and seal the jar using a nonreactive lid.

4. Refrigerate overnight, shaking the jar once or twice after mixing.

A CLOSER LOOK

This is a simple pickling style that can be used for many vegetables. Substitute Napa cabbage, daikon, radishes, or turnips to make a similar pickle on the fly.

SWEET PICKLED CUCUMBERS

MAKES 2 CUPS

Just as American pickles are made in both salty and sweet varieties, so are Japanese pickles. This sweet version is quick and easy, leaving you with snappy morsels of cucumber that pair wonderfully with warm rice, poultry, and fish.

PREP TIME: 10 minutes, plus overnight resting time
COOK TIME: 5 minutes
CURING TIME: 10 hours

4 Japanese pickling cucumbers
1 1/3 tablespoons pickling salt
1/2 cup water, divided
1 1/4 cups rice vinegar
3 tablespoons sugar
1 dried chile pepper
1/2 teaspoon peppercorns

1. Wash the cucumbers and trim both ends off. Cut the cucumbers lengthwise and place in a small dish where they can all lay relatively flat. Rub them with the salt and pour 1/4 cup of water over them. Cover the cucumbers with a plate or other small dish to weigh them down, and leave them overnight or up to 24 hours at room temperature.

2. Rinse the cucumbers under cool water and leave them in the open air until the surface is completely dry.

3. In a nonreactive pot, mix the remaining ingredients, including the remaining 1/4 cup water. Bring the mixture to a boil, turn off the heat, and cool to room temperature.

4. Pack the cucumbers into a quart jar, pressing them down tightly in the bottom. Pour the cooled marinade over the cucumbers. Close the jar with a nonreactive lid and refrigerate. Serve the following day, or store for up to 2 months.

A CLOSER LOOK

If you like the taste of Japanese pickles, you may want to invest in a Japanese pickling crock. However, if you are not there yet, nesting Pyrex glass dishes work well for weighing down these types of pickles. Place the items to be pickled in a large dish, and then on top, add a slightly smaller dish. The rimmed sides make it easy to add weight, and the close sizes of the dishes ensure fairly even pressure.

PICKLED CUCUMBERS AND CABBAGE

MAKES 2 CUPS

If you are tired of eating cucumbers on their own, throw in some cabbage, and you have an entirely new pickle. Ginger is used here to provide the flavoring, and if you chop quickly, you can have this in the refrigerator and weighted in under 5 minutes.

PREP TIME: 5 minutes
CURING TIME: 1 to 3 hours

2 Japanese cucumbers
1 cup Napa cabbage, cut into 2-inch pieces
1 teaspoon ginger
1½ teaspoon salt

1. Remove the ends from the cucumbers and discard. Slice the cucumbers, and mix them with the cabbage, ginger, and salt.

2. Transfer the mixture to a wide mouth jar, pressing firmly to fit it in the jar. Add a narrow, tall jelly jar filled with water and sealed to weigh it down.

3. Refrigerate the cucumbers and cabbage, and serve within 3 hours.

CUCUMBER AND WAKAME PICKLES

MAKES 2 CUPS

This crisp and refreshing pickle adds wakame, a type of seaweed, which contributes its unique texture and flavor. Serve it the following day for the best flavor. Be sure to buy *fueru*-type wakame, which only requires soaking to soften.

PREP TIME: 10 minutes, plus cooling time
CURING TIME: 12 to 24 hours

2 Japanese pickling cucumbers
½ cup sliced daikon
2 tablespoons dried wakame
½ cup rice vinegar
1 (2-inch) square kombu, cut into 3 or 4 pieces
1 teaspoon pickling salt
1 tablespoon sugar
¼ cup water

1. Pack the prepared vegetables and the wakame into a zippered plastic bag.

2. In a small nonreactive pot, combine the remaining ingredients and bring them to a boil, stirring to dissolve the salt and sugar. Turn off the heat and bring the mixture to room temperature. Add this to the bag, seal, and refrigerate for 12 to 24 hours. To serve, pour off the marinade. Eat the pickles within 3 days of preparation.

A CLOSER LOOK

In Japanese quick-pickling, a zippered plastic bag is a good alternative to a jar. Many Japanese pickles do not have the amount of brine that American-style pickles do, making it harder to submerge the pickles and achieve even pickling. If using a bag for a recipe that needs to be weighted, place the bag between two plates and weight the top plate.

PICKLED CABBAGE

MAKES 4 CUPS

Salted and pickled cabbage is used in Asian cooking, both as a stand-alone pickle, and to add flavor to other dishes by cooking it with other ingredients. This is a lightly fermented cabbage with less salt than sauerkraut, meaning it is more prone to spoilage. Because of this, it is typically eaten within a week of pickling.

PREP TIME: 10 minutes
FERMENTATION TIME: 5 days

½ head cabbage (about 1¼ pounds)
1 tablespoon salt
1 (2-inch) square kombu, broken into 3 or 4 pieces
1 tablespoon mirin

1. Cut the cabbage into 3 wedges. In a nonreactive bowl, sprinkle each wedge with the salt. Weigh the cabbage down, and pour ½ cup of water over the cabbage. Cover with a clean kitchen towel and leave at room temperature for 2 days.

2. Drain the cabbage and, using your hands, press out the excess moisture. Place the cabbage back into the bowl and add the kombu. Pour the mirin over the cabbage, cover the cabbage with a weight, and ferment for 3 days at room temperature. When slightly soured, transfer the cabbage to the refrigerator. Eat within 1 week of pickling.

MISO-PICKLED VEGETABLES

MAKES 1 PINT

Miso-pickled vegetables are salty and quite flavorful, especially considering their short pickling time. In just one or two days you can transform ordinary, bland vegetables into near-instant pickles. And the best part: you can continue to reuse the miso to make more pickles as soon as you remove yours from it.

PREP TIME: 5 minutes
CURING TIME: 24 hours

1 pound celery, turnips, radish, daikon, or a combination, divided

½ cup miso paste, divided

1 tablespoon mirin

1 tablespoon sake

1. Prepare the vegetables by cutting them into small, thin pieces about ¼-inch thick.

2. Mix together the miso paste with the mirin and the sake.

3. In a pint jar, spoon in about ¼ cup of the miso paste. Add the vegetables, followed by ⅛ cup of miso and the rest of the vegetables. Cover the top of the vegetables with the remaining ⅛ cup of miso so that none are visible on the top. Cover the jar with a piece of plastic wrap and leave at room temperature.

4. After 24 hours, take a vegetable out, rinse it off, and taste it. If it is to your liking, take the pickles out. If not, leave for an additional 24 hours.

5. To serve, rinse the pickles. These pickles are best within 24 hours of preparation, but they will keep for up to 3 days refrigerated. In between batches, store the miso in the refrigerator.

BRAN PICKLES

MAKES 2 CUPS

The crown jewel of Japanese pickling, bran pickles are time-intensive but worth it. From preparing your pickling bed, testing your pickles, and maintaining the pickling bed, they are simply a lot of work. It is easy to see why these types of pickles, at one time prepared in every household, have fallen by the wayside. However, if you want to experience Japanese pickling at its finest, you should definitely try your hand at these traditional pickles. You will need a small pickling crock or other wide, deep nonreactive dish to make this pickle.

PREP TIME: 30 minutes, plus 1 to 2 weeks for the pickling bed
FERMENTATION TIME: 5 days

⅓ cup pickling salt
1¼ cups water
1 tablespoon miso
½ slice white bread
1 (3-inch) square kombu
1 pound wheat, oat, or rice bran, divided
1 (1-inch) piece of ginger, peeled and cut into small pieces
1 cup mixed vegetables for pickling (cucumbers, daikon, Chinese cabbage, celery, carrots, turnips, green bell pepper)
Extra salt, for rubbing vegetables

1. Prepare the pickling bed by first mixing the salt and water, stirring until the salt is dissolved. Mix the miso together with the water, stirring to combine. Break the bread into small pieces and add this to the water.

2. Wipe the kombu with a damp towel and cut into several pieces using kitchen shears.

3. In the pickling container, add ⅓ of the bran to the bottom, followed by ⅓ of the pickling-bread liquid. Mix well with your hand. Add another ⅓ of bran, followed by ⅓ of the pickling-bread liquid. Do this one more time until all of the bran and pickling liquid are used.

4. Add in the kombu and ginger, and mix well.

5. Rub a couple vegetables (cucumbers, daikon) with salt and bury them in the pickling bed. Pat the bran mixture down firmly with your hands. These are test pickles, so they can be scraps of vegetables, as you will not eat these.

6. Use a wet cloth to wipe the inner rim of the pickling container clean. Cover the pickling bed with a lid or cloth and place in a cool location.

7. After 1 to 3 days, remove the vegetables and discard them. Do this 2 or 3 times and then replace the scraps with vegetables for pickling. Leave the vegetables for 1 to 3 days, then taste them. If they taste good with a well-balanced pickled flavor, they are ready to eat. If not, discard them and try again, being sure not to leave any vegetables in the bed for more than 3 days. Every time you take vegetables out, stir the bed well to aerate the bran, and be sure to wipe the inner rim with a damp, clean cloth.

Continued

8. Once your bed is producing pickles that taste good, keep it active by stirring it every day or two, and always replacing the vegetables after 3 days. It typically takes at least 1 to 2 weeks to get the pickling bed performing well and producing pickles that taste really good.

A CLOSER LOOK

Customarily, these are made using rice bran, but since this is not widely available in the United States, wheat and oat bran are also recommended here.

BRAN PICKLING TIPS

Bran pickling is typically started in spring and early summer, as it can take up to one month to obtain a good flavor from the pickling bed. Be sure to get yours going with plenty of time to take advantage of the endless summer pickling opportunities. Here are some tips to keep in mind when bran pickling:

- Firm vegetables such as carrots and daikon need more time in the pickling bed to achieve full flavor. To combat this and speed up pickling, cut them into small pieces. Other vegetables such as cucumbers, eggplants, and celery can be pickled whole.

- Always rub vegetables lightly with salt before burying in the pickling bed to help aid in the pickling.

- Don't leave any vegetables in the pickling bed, as this can cause sourness. Always be sure to stir the bed well and inspect for missed vegetables. If your bed does become sour, add a tablespoon or two of mustard powder to neutralize the bed.

- Keep it cool. In Japan, pickling beds were traditionally kept in the floor, where temperatures remain cooler. A root cellar or basement is an ideal location—just don't forget about it.

- If mold appears on the pickling bed, remove it promptly from the surface, and wipe the inner rim clean.

- In theory, if you keep your pickling bed well-maintained, it can be reused year after year. To do this, store in the refrigerator as noted above. Bring the bed to room temperature, and add additional aromatics such as more kombu, ginger, garlic, mustard powder, or chile pepper. Begin the same process of testing as when you started pickling.

VIETNAMESE PICKLED DAIKON AND CARROTS

MAKES 2 CUPS

This quick pickle is exceedingly fresh, and adds a nice crunch to a sandwich or can simply be eaten on its own. This type of pickle is most commonly made by cutting the daikon into matchsticks for convenient stuffing into sandwiches and rolls, but feel free to prepare the vegetables however you like best.

PREP TIME: 10 minutes, plus 30 minutes
   resting time
CURING TIME: 2 hours

1 carrot, peeled and cut into matchsticks
1 pound daikon, peeled and cut into matchsticks
1½ teaspoons salt
2 tablespoons sugar
½ cup water
½ cup rice vinegar

1. Toss the carrot and daikon with the salt in a small bowl. Set aside for 30 minutes, then drain the vegetables, pressing as much excess water from them as possible. Pack the vegetables into a pint jar.

2. In a small bowl, mix the sugar, water, and vinegar until dissolved. Pour the liquid over the vegetables, cover, and refrigerate for 2 hours before serving.

CHINESE FERMENTED MUSTARD GREENS

Fermented mustard greens are a cornerstone flavor of many Chinese dishes. Like many other ferments that boast complex, rich flavors, they are fairly simple to make. Select mature mustard greens for this recipe, as their thick, fibrous stems are desirable here.

PREP TIME: 10 minutes, plus 12 hours drying
and 30 minutes rest time
FERMENTATION TIME: 10 days

1½ pounds mustard greens
2 tablespoons pickling salt, divided
½ teaspoon Sichuan peppercorns
3 cups water

1. Wash the mustard greens well and allow them to air-dry for about 12 hours, or until they begin to wilt.

2. In a large bowl, combine the mustard greens with 1 tablespoon of salt and the peppercorns. Rub the salt into the greens and let them sit for 30 minutes until they begin to lose some water. Squeeze out as much of this water as possible, and transfer the greens to a sanitized jar. Add the remaining 1 tablespoon of salt to the jar.

3. Bring the water to a boil and pour the water over the greens. Weigh down the greens so that they are submerged in the jar. Cover the jar loosely with a nonreactive lid once the brine is cool, and store in a room temperature location.

4. After 10 days, the greens will have taken on a bright green hue, signifying that they are finished. Remove the weight, close the jar tightly with a non-reactive lid, and transfer the jar to the refrigerator, where the greens will keep for several months.

A CLOSER LOOK

When needed, remove small amounts of greens to season dishes, but be careful how you do it. You don't want to introduce new bacteria into the jar, so always use a clean utensil devoid of oil or any other substance to prevent potential contamination.

DAIKON KIMCHI

MAKES 1 PINT

Daikon kimchi is a popular form of kimchi in Korean cuisine, second only to the classic cabbage kimchi. The satisfying crunch of the firm radish and a generous portion of ground dried hot pepper makes this one to have in small, bite-size servings along with a cooling portion of rice. Choose a firm, large daikon when making this recipe for the best results, and if you have some leftover, use it for one of the many other daikon recipes in this book.

PREP TIME: 10 minutes, plus 30 minutes resting time
FERMENTATION TIME: 3 to 4 days

1¼ pounds daikon, peeled and cut into
    1-inch cubes

1½ teaspoons pickling salt

1 tablespoon sugar

2 garlic clove, minced

1 tablespoon Korean ground dried hot pepper

2 scallions, cut into 1-inch pieces

1-inch piece of ginger, grated

1 teaspoon white vinegar

1. In a small bowl, combine the daikon, salt, and sugar. Let rest at room temperature for 30 minutes. Strain the juice in the bowl, reserving it for later use.

2. Mix the garlic, hot pepper, scallions, ginger, and vinegar together with the daikon. Pack the mixture into a clean pint jar, pressing down firmly as you go to remove air bubbles. Pour the reserved brine over the radishes to cover. Cap the jar with a nonreactive lid, and leave the kimchi at room temperature for 3 to 4 days. Transfer to the refrigerator where it will keep for several months.

8

CHUTNEYS, SALSAS, AND RELISHES

When fruits and vegetables are diced or pureed before pickling, they can transform into something new altogether. These versatile pickled condiments are the perfect solution for topping a burger, spooning over a chicken breast or pork chop, or scooping up with a tortilla chip. You'll find a mix of savory and sweet chutneys, salsas, and relishes in this chapter, giving you an opportunity to add pickles to just about every meal.

PLUM CHUTNEY

Plums pair nicely with pork and chicken, making this a great addition to the dinner table. Use fully ripe plums for this recipe, as they will impart the best flavor to this thickened, spiced chutney. Ginger, red chili pepper flakes, garlic, and mustard seeds all add to the complexity of this chutney. If you like spice, add a bit more chili pepper flakes, or dice a chile pepper and add it to the mixture.

PREP TIME: 15 minutes
COOK TIME: 45 minutes
PROCESSING TIME: 10 minutes

½ cup brown sugar

½ cup sugar

½ cup white vinegar

1¾ cups purple plums, cored and chopped

2 tablespoons chopped onion

½ cup golden raisins

1 teaspoon pickling salt

1 teaspoon mustard seeds

1 tablespoon crystallized ginger

1 garlic clove, crushed

½ teaspoon red chili pepper flakes

1. In a nonreactive pot, combine the sugars and vinegar and heat until simmering, stirring to dissolve the sugars. Add all the remaining ingredients and stir well to mix. Bring the mixture to a boil and turn down the heat to simmer. Cook for 45 minutes, until the chutney begins to thicken.

2. Ladle the chutney into the half-pint jars, leaving ¼ inch of headspace. Cap the jars using two-piece canning lids.

3. Process the chutney in a boiling-water bath for 10 minutes, or refrigerate.

MANGO CHUTNEY

MAKES 2 HALF-PINTS

Bring the taste of the islands to your table with this quick and simple chutney. At once hot and sweet, this chutney pairs well with turkey and pork dishes. Curry powder brings complexity to the flavor, while pepper flakes add heat to complement the sweetness—and a bit of color, too.

PREP TIME: 15 minutes
COOK TIME: 1 hour
PROCESSING TIME: 10 minutes

2 mangoes, ripe but not soft
1 cup white vinegar
1 cup brown sugar
1 teaspoon hot pepper flakes
¼ teaspoon pickling salt
1½ teaspoons curry powder
¼ cup golden raisins

1. Mix together all the ingredients except the raisins in a bowl. Cover with plastic wrap and allow to sit overnight at room temperature.

2. The next day, transfer the chutney to a non-reactive pot. Add the raisins, bring the mixture to a simmer, and cook until thickened, about 1 hour.

3. Ladle the chutney into half-pint jars, and cap using two-piece canning lids. Process for 10 minutes in a boiling-water bath, or refrigerate.

A CLOSER LOOK

A mango has an elliptical pit, making its prep work kind of tricky. First skin the mango, then cut two large pieces from each side, and two smaller pieces from the opposite sides. Dice these pieces. It helps to select firm mangoes, as they are easier to work with.

8

CHUTNEYS, SALSAS, AND RELISHES

RHUBARB CHUTNEY

Fresh rhubarb is a welcome addition in late spring, when locally grown fresh produce is slowly becoming available again. However, if you don't have a supply of fresh rhubarb, frozen works just as well. The sourness of rhubarb plays well in chutney where it shines among onions, ginger, and a little spice. Try it alongside any meat or poultry.

PREP TIME: 15 minutes
COOK TIME: 30 minutes
PROCESSING TIME: 10 minutes

1 cup apple cider vinegar
¾ cup brown sugar
1½ cups diced rhubarb
1 cup chopped red onions
1 tablespoon minced ginger
¼ teaspoon red chili pepper flakes
¼ teaspoon pickling salt
1 cinnamon stick
½ cup dried cranberries

1. In a nonreactive pot, heat the vinegar and sugar, stirring to dissolve the sugar. Add all the remaining ingredients. Bring the mixture to a boil, then turn down the heat to simmer the chutney until thickened, about 30 minutes.

2. Remove the cinnamon stick and ladle the chutney into prepared jars. Cap the jars using two-piece canning lids.

3. Process the jars for 10 minutes in a boiling-water bath, or refrigerate.

CHUTNEYS, SALSAS, AND RELISHES

APPLE CHUTNEY

Apple chutney pairs wonderfully with pork as a departure from the typical applesauce. Combining spice with sweetness here successfully produces a deliciously thick and complex chutney. A medley of peppers gives it a striking appearance, and a healthy dose of ginger delivers spice. For optimal flavor, use tart apples such as Granny Smiths.

PREP TIME: 15 minutes
COOK TIME: 1 hour
PROCESSING TIME: 10 minutes

2 cups chopped apples
¼ cup chopped onion
¼ cup chopped red bell pepper
2 hot red peppers, seeded and diced
½ cup golden raisins
1 cup brown sugar
1 tablespoon ground ginger
2 teaspoons whole mustard seeds
2 teaspoons ground allspice
½ teaspoon pickling salt
1 garlic clove
1 cup white vinegar

1. In a nonreactive pot, combine all the ingredients. Bring the mixture to a boil, turn down the heat, and simmer until thickened. Stir frequently as the chutney thickens to prevent scorching. It will take about 1 hour for the chutney to thicken.

2. Ladle the hot chutney into jars, leaving ½ inch of headspace. Cap the jars with two-piece canning lids.

3. Process in a boiling-water bath for 10 minutes, or refrigerate.

8

CHUTNEYS, SALSAS, AND RELISHES

LACTO-FERMENTED CRANBERRY CHUTNEY

MAKES 1 QUART

Skip the canned cranberry sauce next Thanksgiving, and make this simple chutney instead. The best part is that it's loaded with healthy probiotics—just what you need after a big meal. Plan on making this at least 2 days before serving to allow for plenty of fermentation time.

PREP TIME: 10 minutes
COOK TIME: none
FERMENTATION TIME: 2 days

1 pound fresh or frozen cranberries
½ cup honey
1 teaspoon sea salt
⅓ cup kombucha (non-pasteurized) or whey
½ cup white grape juice
1 teaspoon cinnamon
Juice of 1 orange
2 teaspoons orange zest

1. Combine all the ingredients except the orange zest in a blender or food processor. Process until the cranberries are well chopped, yet still chunky. Transfer the mixture to a quart jar and mix in the orange zest.

2. Cover with a nonreactive lid and leave the jar at room temperature to ferment for 2 days. Transfer to the refrigerator where its flavors will continue to develop.

A CLOSER LOOK

Fresh cranberries are harvested annually, and typically appear at the supermarket only in the weeks leading up to Thanksgiving and Christmas. If you are a fan of these bitter nutritional powerhouses, stock up by buying a couple bags for the freezer, and take them out as needed throughout the year.

CHUTNEYS, SALSAS, AND RELISHES

8

LACTO-FERMENTED PINEAPPLE CHUTNEY

Unlike some chutneys that focus on heat, this one is entirely sweet. Using just a handful of ingredients, you can turn the tropical pineapple into the perfect topping for meat, poultry, and even yogurt through this simple fermentation process. Cilantro makes this chutney a bit savory, while ginger and lime juice round out the condiment.

PREP TIME: 20 minutes
COOK TIME: none
FERMENTATION TIME: 2 to 3 days

1 pineapple, diced
1 bunch cilantro, minced
1 (2-inch) piece of ginger, peeled and grated
2 teaspoons pickling salt
Juice of 1 lime
½ cup kombucha (non-pasteurized) or whey
½ cup water

1. In a nonreactive bowl, mix the pineapple, cilantro, ginger, and salt. Pack into a quart jar. Use a spoon to pack the pineapple down into the jar, pressing to release some of its juices.

2. Mix together the lime juice, kombucha or whey, and water. Add the mixture to the jar. Press the pineapple into the liquid, which should cover the chutney by about 1 inch. If it doesn't, add a bit more water until it does.

3. Cover the jar with a nonreactive lid, and leave it at room temperature to ferment for 2 to 3 days. Transfer the pineapple to the refrigerator where its flavors will continue to develop.

A CLOSER LOOK

A pineapple should smell sweet when purchasing. The best place to check its aroma is the base. If it lacks a scent, leave it at the store. Because a pineapple does not become sweeter after picking, it is important to pick one that is both firm and has a good smell at the time of purchase.

PICO DE GALLO

MAKES 1½ PINTS

A fresh salsa that is both quick and delicious, pico de gallo is a mainstay in Mexican cuisine. If you can, use Roma or other firm plum tomatoes so the salsa doesn't end up overly watery. Spoon the finished pico de gallo over tacos, nachos, or just eat it by the spoonful—it's really that good.

PREP TIME: 15 minutes, plus 15 minutes
   resting time
COOK TIME: none

1 pound ripe plum tomatoes, diced
1 teaspoon salt
½ white onion, peeled and diced
1 jalapeño pepper, seeds and stem removed, diced
¼ cup chopped cilantro leaves
Juice of ½ lime

1. Toss the tomatoes with the salt, and place them in a colander to drain for about 15 minutes.

2. Mix the drained tomatoes with the rest of the ingredients. Refrigerate for up to 3 days.

A CLOSER LOOK

Jalapeños are the traditional chile pepper used in salsa in Mexican cuisine. Depending on the season though, they can vary considerably in heat, with winter chiles milder than those grown during the hotter months. Taste the chiles before using and, if desired, add an extra to suit your preference.

8

CHUTNEYS, SALSAS, AND RELISHES

SPICY TOMATO SALSA

Tomatoes are an easy addition to the garden, and when you have a large harvest, there is no better use for them than canning them up in salsa to enjoy all year. Put an end to store-bought salsa with this home-canned recipe that may just rival your favorite brand. Similar to a fresh pico de gallo, this salsa has a short ingredient list, but delivers on flavor. Adjust the bell and chile pepper ratio to your desired heat level.

PREP TIME: 20 minutes
COOK TIME: 15 minutes
PROCESSING TIME: 15 minutes

6 cups chopped plum tomatoes
1 cup chopped onion
4 cups chopped chile and bell peppers
¾ cup white or apple cider vinegar
2 teaspoons pickling salt

1. In a nonreactive pot, combine all the ingredients and bring them to a boil. Turn down the heat and simmer the salsa for 10 minutes.

2. Pack the salsa into pint jars, leaving ½ inch of headspace. Process in a boiling-water bath for 15 minutes.

3. Store the jars in a cool, dark, and dry location for up to 1 year. Once opened, the salsa will keep for 1 week.

A CLOSER LOOK

When cutting a large amount of chiles to make a salsa, be sure to wear kitchen gloves as the oils from the chiles can cause a lot of pain on your hands, and anywhere else on your body you touch as well. If you don't have kitchen gloves, just fit a couple of plastic sandwich bags over your hands to prevent skin contact with the chiles.

PEACH AND MANGO SALSA

MAKES 1½ PINTS

If you want a taste of summer, here it is! This salsa, featuring appearances from some of summer's best bounty, is loaded with flavor and ready to treat your taste buds right. This salsa pairs well with fish as in Grilled Fish Tacos with Peach and Mango Salsa (page 152), or simply pair with tortilla chips to be transported to a sunny summer day no matter what time of year.

PREP TIME: 15 minutes
COOK TIME: none

4 peaches, peeled and diced
1 mango, peeled and diced
3 Roma or other plum tomatoes, diced
½ red onion, peeled and diced
1 red bell pepper, diced
2 jalapeño or serrano peppers, diced
1 garlic clove, minced
Juice of 1 lime
1 tablespoon honey

In a nonreactive bowl, mix all the ingredients. Use immediately, or refrigerate for up to 3 days before using.

TRY INSTEAD

With a fresh recipe like this one, which is not meant to be canned or fermented, you have plenty of versatility when it comes to substituting ingredients. If you don't like mango, for example, stick with all peach instead. If you'd prefer more heat, add in some extra chiles, or if you'd like to experiment with bolder flavor, add ½ teaspoon of cumin, which goes well with peaches.

LACTO-FERMENTED MANGO SALSA

MAKES 1 QUART

Mango salsa on its own is fabulous, but with some gut-nourishing probiotics it is even better. Prep this ferment quickly one afternoon, and it will be ready for dinner the following day. Simple and sweet, this pairs well with salads, fish, and chicken, or just enjoy it on its own by the spoonful.

PREP TIME: 10 minutes
COOK TIME: none
FERMENTATION TIME: 1 day

3 mangos, peeled and diced

3 garlic cloves, diced

1 shallot, diced

2 tablespoons diced red onion

2 tablespoons kombucha (non-pasteurized) or whey

1½ teaspoons pickling salt

¼ cup cilantro leaves

1 tablespoon freshly squeezed lime juice

1. Combine all of the ingredients in a quart jar, and press lightly to submerge the mango in liquid.

2. Cover with a nonreactive lid and leave the jar at room temperature to ferment for up to 24 hours. Transfer the salsa to the refrigerator where its flavors will continue to develop. Eat within 2 weeks.

TOMATILLO SALSA

MAKES 2 PINTS

Green salsa is a wonderful addition to your menu, as it can be used in the same way as tomato salsa. This recipe gives you the option to can it or transfer to the refrigerator to eat straightaway.

PREP TIME: 15 minutes
COOK TIME: 15 minutes
PROCESSING TIME: 15 minutes

2½ pounds tomatillos,
    husks removed and chopped
2 cups white onions, diced
4 jalapeño peppers
3 garlic cloves, minced
¾ cup white vinegar
2½ teaspoons pickling salt

1. In a nonreactive pot, combine all the ingredients. Bring the mixture to a boil, then simmer for 15 minutes.

2. Using an immersion blender, process the salsa until it is coarsely puréed.

3. Ladle the salsa into prepared pint jars, leaving ½ inch of headspace. Cap the jars with two-piece canning lids.

4. Process the jars in a boiling-water bath for 15 minutes and then store them in a cool, dark, and dry location for up to 1 year. Once opened, the salsa will keep, refrigerated, for 2 weeks.

TRY INSTEAD

If you don't have an immersion blender, a traditional blender or food processor works well too. Be sure to work in batches, and be careful when working with the hot salsa to prevent burns. Also, when blending the salsa, purée to your preferred texture. If desired, leave it chunky.

TOMATO KETCHUP

MAKES 3 PINTS

This is not the ketchup you buy in the store: instead, this flavor-forward tomato ketchup boasts plenty of bite. Store-bought ketchups are laden with salt and sugar, while this ketchup relies most heavily on ripe tomato flavor and the subtle notes of cloves, mustard seeds, allspice, and cinnamon.

PREP TIME: 20 minutes
COOK TIME: 2 hours
PROCESSING TIME: 15 minutes

10 pounds of Roma or paste tomatoes, coarsely chopped
1 cup diced onion
4 garlic cloves
2 cups apple cider vinegar
1½ teaspoons pickling salt
½ cup packed brown sugar
¾ teaspoon cayenne pepper
1 tablespoon mustard seeds
1 tablespoon black peppercorns
1 tablespoon whole allspice
1 cinnamon stick, broken

1. In a nonreactive pot, combine the tomatoes, onion, and garlic cloves. Heat the tomato mixture to boiling, reduce the heat, and simmer uncovered for 30 minutes until it is soft.

2. Remove the pot from the heat and transfer the tomatoes to a food mill or sieve. Process the tomatoes and onion, removing the seeds and skins. Return the tomato pulp to the original pot.

3. Add the vinegar, salt, brown sugar, and cayenne pepper to the tomato purée. Using a small scrap of cheesecloth, create a spice pouch and pack it with the mustard seeds, black peppercorns, allspice, and cinnamon stick. Tie the bag shut using kitchen twine and place it in the purée.

4. Bring the mixture to a boil, then reduce the heat to a simmer until it has reduced to a thickened ketchup consistency, about 90 minutes.

5. Remove the spice pouch from the ketchup, ladle the ketchup into prepared jars, leaving ½ inch headspace. Process in a boiling-water bath for 15 minutes.

6. Store the ketchup in a cool, dry, and dark location for up to 1 year.

TRY INSTEAD

If you don't have a food mill or sieve, remove the tomato skins by cutting an "X" in the skin. Blanch for about 30 seconds in boiling water, then immediately put in an ice-bath. The skins should slip off easily. Cut the tomatoes in half and scrape out as many seeds as you can.

BLUEBERRY KETCHUP

Instead of eating these juicy morsels fresh, try this simple and fun recipe to liven up everything from hamburgers to barbecued chicken. A fresh recipe not designed for canning, this unexpected condiment can be easily whipped up at midday and will be ready and chilled by dinner.

PREP TIME: 15 minutes
COOK TIME: 30 minutes

2 cups blueberries
1 shallot, diced
1 cup sugar
⅓ cup red wine vinegar
1 tablespoon lime juice
1 tablespoon minced ginger
¼ teaspoon salt

1. In a nonreactive pot, combine all the ingredients. Bring the mixture to a boil, reduce the heat, and simmer, stirring until the sugar dissolves. Using the back of a spoon, mash the blueberries as you stir.

2. Continue to cook the ketchup until it is thickened, about 30 minutes. Ladle it into a pint jar, refrigerate until cold, and serve.

GOOSEBERRY KETCHUP

If you are one of the lucky ones with access to gooseberries, you have got to try making this ketchup. Use red or white gooseberries to make this ketchup or, if you can't find them, substitute currants instead. If you don't have access to either, consider adding a plant to your yard to boost your edible bounty.

PREP TIME: 5 minutes
COOK TIME: 40 minutes
PROCESSING TIME: 10 minutes

1 pound gooseberries
1 cup sugar
1 cup apple cider vinegar
1 garlic clove, minced
1 teaspoon ground ginger
1 teaspoon ground allspice
½ teaspoon cayenne pepper

1. In a nonreactive pot, combine the gooseberries, sugar, and vinegar. Bring to a boil, reduce the heat, and simmer until the gooseberries are softened, about 10 minutes.

2. Transfer the mixture to a food mill and process it, removing the seeds and skins. Return the ketchup to the original pot. Add the ginger, allspice, and cayenne pepper, and cook the ketchup until it is thickened, about 20 minutes.

3. Ladle the ketchup into a 1 pint jar or 2 half-pints, and cap the jars using two-piece canning lids. Process in a boiling-water bath for 10 minutes.

4. Store the jars in a cool, dark, dry location for up to 1 year.

8

CHUTNEYS, SALSAS, AND RELISHES

RED AND GREEN CUCUMBER RELISH

MAKES 4 HALF-PINTS

This relish is just perfect for scooping onto a hot dog on a hot summer day. Can this all-purpose cucumber relish, and have plenty to go around all year, or give a half-pint to a friend. Draining the relish first by soaking it with ice ensures that it's packed with crunch, even after months of storage in a jar.

PREP TIME: 15 minutes, 5 hours resting time
PROCESSING TIME: 10 minutes

1½ pounds pickling cucumbers, finely diced
¾ cup red sweet peppers, finely diced
¼ cup onions, peeled and diced
3 tablespoons pickling salt
1½ cups apple cider vinegar
¼ cup sugar
1 teaspoon mustard seed
1 teaspoon turmeric

1. In a large nonreactive bowl, combine the cucumbers, peppers, and onion. Toss with the salt. Cover the vegetables with 1 cup of water and 1 cup of ice cubes. Let stand at room temperature for 4 hours. Use a colander to drain the salted water away from the vegetables. Add 1 more cup of ice to the top of the vegetables and let stand for an additional hour. Drain and discard the water again.

2. Put the vinegar in a nonreactive pot. Add the sugar, mustard seed, and turmeric and bring the mixture to a boil. Immediately add the cucumber mixture and bring the liquid back to a boil.

3. Ladle the relish into jars, leaving ½ inch of headspace. Cap the jars using two-piece canning lids. Process in a boiling-water bath for 10 minutes.

4. Store the jars in a cool, dry, dark location for up to 1 year.

SPICY ZUCCHINI RELISH

It's no surprise that the zucchini is often a stand-in for the cucumber, and here is another pickle where you would be hard-pressed to differentiate between the two. Similar to a cucumber relish, this simple vegetable mixture brings a spicy edge to an otherwise ordinary relish.

PREP TIME: 15 minutes
COOK TIME: 40 minutes
PROCESSING TIME: 10 minutes

2 cups finely chopped green bell pepper
1 cup finely chopped jalapeño pepper
1 cup grated onion
3 cups grated zucchini
2 cups apple cider vinegar, divided
1 cup sugar
1 tablespoon pickling salt
1 tablespoon mustard seed

1. In a nonreactive pot, bring the green bell pepper, jalapeño pepper, onion, zucchini, and 1 cup of vinegar to a boil. Turn down the heat and simmer the mixture until it begins to reduce, about 30 minutes.

2. Drain the vegetables in a colander and return them to the pot. Add the remaining 1 cup vinegar, sugar, salt, and mustard seed. Bring the mixture to a boil, turn down the heat, and simmer for 5 minutes.

3. Ladle the relish into jars, leaving ½ inch of headspace. Cap the jars using two-piece canning lids. Process the jars for 10 minutes in a boiling-water bath.

A CLOSER LOOK

Unless you select really small zucchini, they are likely to have a lot of seeds. For relish, you don't want any seeds, so be sure to cut away the zucchini's seedy inner layer before dicing.

CHUTNEYS, SALSAS, AND RELISHES

CORN RELISH

Can up a bit of summer with this corn relish that highlights one of the season's sweetest treats. Serve it as a side, mix it with rice, or heap it on a burger to enjoy this piquant treat.

PREP TIME: 10 minutes
COOK TIME: 15 minutes
PROCESSING TIME: 15 minutes

4 cups fresh corn
1 cup diced red bell peppers
1 cup diced green bell peppers
1 cup diced red onions
2 tablespoons minced garlic
1 teaspoon pickling salt
1 teaspoon ground cumin
2 cups apple cider vinegar
⅔ cup sugar
½ teaspoon red chili pepper flakes

1. In a nonreactive pot, combine all the ingredients. Bring the mixture to a boil, reduce the heat, and simmer for 10 minutes.

2. Ladle the salsa into jars, leaving ½ inch of headspace. Cap the jars using two-piece canning lids, and process in a boiling-water bath for 15 minutes.

3. Store the jars in a cool, dry, dark location for up to 1 year.

LACTO-FERMENTED CARROT RELISH

MAKES 1 QUART

Add this bright and nutrient-dense relish to your favorite salads, or serve it as a side dish with Asian-inspired meals. With a strong ginger overtone, this is one relish you definitely want included in your repertoire.

PREP TIME: 15 minutes
FERMENTATION TIME: 14 days

2 pounds carrots, peeled and shredded
1½ cups shredded Chinese cabbage
2 tablespoons peeled and finely shredded onion
1 tablespoon grated ginger
2 cups water
1 tablespoon pickling salt

1. In a nonreactive bowl, mix the carrots, cabbage, onion, and ginger. Pack into a quart jar.

2. In a measuring cup, stir the water and salt until dissolved. Pour over the vegetables, pressing them down with a spoon so that they are completely covered with the liquid.

3. Close the jar using a nonreactive lid or a plastic food-safe zippered bag filled with brine, using the same ratio of 2 cups water per 1 tablespoon pickling salt. Place the jar in a room temperature location and ferment for 14 days, or until fermentation stops.

4. Transfer the carrot relish to the refrigerator, where it will keep at least 1 month.

A CLOSER LOOK

If you plan on pickling regularly, investing in a microplane grater to prepare ginger is a great idea. With smaller holes than a traditional grater, a microplane grater creates a near purée of ginger, perfect for mixing into ferments where large chunks of ginger are not desirable.

GREEN TOMATO RELISH

MAKES 5 HALF-PINTS

If you have access to a couple pounds of green tomatoes come fall, making this relish is a great way to put them to work for you. Use this relish like you would cucumber relish, and slather it on sandwiches, use it in dipping sauces, or save it for hot dogs.

PREP TIME: 10 minutes
COOK TIME: 15 minutes, plus 4 hours resting time
PROCESSING TIME: 10 minutes

2½ pounds green tomatoes, diced
½ cup diced green bell pepper
½ cup diced onion
2 tablespoons pickling salt
1 cup white vinegar
¾ cup sugar
1½ teaspoons celery seed
1½ teaspoons mustard seed

1. In a nonreactive pot, combine the tomatoes, pepper, onion, and pickling salt. Let stand at room temperature for 4 hours. Bring the vegetables to a boil and simmer for 5 minutes. Drain the vegetables in a sieve or fine strainer, pressing out as much of the liquid as possible. Return them to the pot.

2. In another nonreactive pot, combine the vinegar, sugar, celery seed, and mustard seed. Bring this mixture to a boil, reduce the heat, and simmer for 5 minutes. Pour this liquid over the vegetables and bring the mixture to a boil. Reduce the heat and simmer for 5 more minutes.

3. Ladle the relish into jars, leaving ½ inch of headspace. Cap the jars using two-piece canning lids, and process in a boiling-water bath for 10 minutes.

A CLOSER LOOK

Green tomatoes are not typically sold at stores. If you don't grow tomatoes yourself, ask someone who does. Many people simply discard or compost these instead of eating them and are often more than happy to give them away.

LACTO-FERMENTED TOMATILLO SALSA

MAKES 1 PINT

Canning salsa is a no-brainer for winter months when tomatillos are not readily available, but this recipe is meant to be enjoyed fresh from the garden at the height of the growing season. Adding probiotics to your diet is so easy when you can scoop it onto tortillas or spoon it over your favorite tacos. A short fermentation time gives this salsa its healthy edge, and the jalapeños bring a satisfying heat to make this a summer-time favorite.

PREP TIME: 15 minutes
FERMENTATION TIME: 48 hours

1 pound tomatillos, husks removed and coarsely chopped

1 cup white onions, diced

2 jalapeño peppers, stemmed and seeds removed

1 garlic clove, peeled

½ cup minced cilantro

1 tablespoon lime juice

1½ teaspoons pickling salt

2 tablespoons whey

1. In a blender or food processor, combine the tomatillos, onions, jalapeños, garlic, and cilantro. Pulse until pureed. Transfer to a clean pint jar.

2. Stir in the lime juice, salt, and whey. Cover with a nonreactive lid and leave at room temperature to ferment for 48 hours. Transfer to the refrigerator, and store for up to 2 weeks.

PREP TIP

If you don't have a blender or food processor, that's fine. Tomatillo salsa is generally puréed, but that doesn't mean that is the only way to serve it. Simply mince all the vegetables as finely as you can to create a slightly chunkier salsa and proceed to step 2.

8

CHUTNEYS, SALSAS, AND RELISHES

9
COOKING WITH PICKLES

Now that you've pickled a few things, these recipes will help you incorporate your creations into your everyday meals. Add pickles to these and other simple dishes to create complex flavors and truly enjoy the fruits of your labor. These are all quick and easy recipes that do a great job of highlighting the many unique flavors of pickles, while allowing them to mingle with other complementary ingredients to create a cohesive meal.

PICKLED PEACHES AND YOGURT

SERVES 2

Pickled peaches—well, really any sweet pickled fruit—combine wonderfully with yogurt for a quick but lovely meal or snack. To make it a bit more filling, add in a ½ cup of granola. Sweet and tart at the same time, this combination works best with plain yogurt, but if you prefer something a little sweeter, try it with honey yogurt instead.

PREP TIME: 5 minutes

1½ cups plain yogurt
1 cup Pickled Peaches (page 86)

In two bowls, divide the yogurt. Top with the peaches and serve. If desired, drizzle a tablespoon of the pickling liquid over the yogurt as well.

TRY INSTEAD

This combination also works exceedingly well with pickled pears, strawberries, or blueberries. Or, if you prefer to make it a dessert, replace the yogurt with ice cream and top with either pickled peaches or pears.

COOKING WITH PICKLES

9

BLOODY MARY WITH PICKLED VEGETABLES

SERVES 2

A Bloody Mary is the ultimate cocktail that combines both food and drink. Skip the bottled mix and make this yourself using tomato juice, pickle brine, and more for a refreshing and nourishing drink. Garnish the summertime favorite with some of your pickling stock, and you'll have a perfect drink for a guest.

PREP TIME: 10 minutes

Kosher salt

½ lemon

Ice

3 ounces vodka

12 ounces tomato juice

4 dashes hot sauce

4 dashes Worcestershire sauce

4 tablespoons pickling brine

2 Classic Dill Pickles (page 63) or Spicy Dill Pickles (page 64)

2 to 4 Dilly Beans (page 43) or Lacto-Fermented Beans (page 71)

1. On a small plate, pour a thin layer of kosher salt. Rub the lemon across the rims of two highball glasses, and then dip them in the salt. Fill the glasses with ice.

2. Split the vodka between the two glasses and then add the tomato juice evenly to each. Add 2 dashes of hot sauce and Worcestershire sauce to each glass and 2 tablespoons of pickling brine. Squeeze the lemon over each glass, extracting the juice. Stir each glass using a long spoon.

3. Garnish with pickled vegetables and serve.

FRIED PICKLES

SERVES 2 TO 4

A bar favorite, fried pickles are easily accessible at home. Make sure to cut them into spears, as they will absorb the most flavor during marinating, as well as hold onto more of the breading than whole pickles would.

PREP TIME: 20 minutes, plus 30 minutes
  resting time
COOK TIME: 3 to 5 minutes

½ teaspoon garlic powder

½ cup buttermilk or yogurt

Oil for frying

1 cup flour

¼ cup cornmeal

¼ teaspoon salt

¼ teaspoon freshly ground black pepper

1 pint jar Classic Dill Pickles (page 63), Spicy Dill Pickles (page 64), or Garlic Dill Pickles (page 65)

1. Drain the brine from the pickle jar and add the garlic powder and buttermilk to the jar. Shake gently to disperse the buttermilk and let marinate for 30 minutes.

2. Pour oil in a deep pot and heat to 350°F.

3. In a small bowl, mix the flour, cornmeal, salt, and pepper. Remove the pickles from the jar, cut them into spears, and roll them in the flour mixture.

4. Cook the pickles in batches for about 3 to 5 minutes each depending on their size. When they are well-browned, they are done. Depending on the amount of oil used, you may need to flip them halfway through cooking.

5. Remove the pickles using tongs, and drain on a plate lined with paper towels before serving.

A CLOSER LOOK

A candy thermometer is a good tool to have on hand for deep frying to gauge oil temperature. If you don't have one, however, that's okay, too. Heat the oil over medium-high heat and when it begins to shimmer, add a small pinch of flour. If it immediately sizzles away, the oil is ready. If it sits in the oil for a second or two before disappearing, allow it to heat a little longer and then try again.

OLD-FASHIONED POTATO SALAD

SERVES 4 TO 6

Pickles add a welcome tang to potato salad and are a traditional ingredient of old-fashioned potato salads. Take your pick as to the type of dill pickles to include based on your own personal preference and what you have available. For the best flavor, be sure to allow plenty of time for chilling the salad before serving.

PREP TIME: 30 minutes

1½ pounds Yukon gold potatoes

3 hard-boiled eggs

1 celery rib, finely diced

3 to 5 scallions, thinly sliced

1 whole dill pickle, finely diced (Quick Dill Pickles page 36, or Classic Dill Pickles page 63)

¾ cup mayonnaise

2 tablespoons dill pickle brine

2 teaspoons prepared mustard

½ teaspoon salt

¼ teaspoon freshly ground black pepper

1. Place the potatoes in a large pot and cover with water. Bring to a boil and cook for 20 to 30 minutes, until tender. Drain and cool the potatoes under running water. Once cool, peel and cut the potatoes.

2. Place the potatoes in a large bowl, add the eggs, and roughly chop. Add the celery, scallions, and pickles.

3. In another small bowl, mix together the mayonnaise, pickle brine, mustard, salt, and pepper. Add this seasoning mixture to the potato mixture and mix well. Cover and refrigerate for at least 4 hours to chill before serving.

TRY INSTEAD

To cut down on cooking time, cut the potatoes into quarters before boiling. When smaller, the potatoes can typically be cooked in the same pot with the eggs for about 10 minutes. Test with a fork to confirm that they are done before draining the water.

PICKLED BEET, FETA, AND WALNUT SALAD

SERVES 2

Pickled beets are a wonderfully sweet addition to a salad. When paired with walnuts and feta cheese, the salad becomes a filling meal. Whip this up for a hearty lunch or light dinner, and enjoy eating your home-pickled beets one jar at a time. Because the brine makes the dressing, this quick-prep salad can be on the table in just a few minutes.

PREP TIME: 5 minutes

6 packed cups baby greens (any combination of kale, arugula, lettuces, bok choy, chard)

1 cup Pickled Beets (page 42)

½ cup walnut pieces

2 ounces crumbled feta cheese

1 tablespoon extra-virgin olive oil, divided

3 tablespoons pickled beet brine, divided

Salt

Freshly ground black pepper

1. On two large plates, split the salad greens in half. If your pickled beets are whole, slice them into ¼-inch-thick slices and arrange them on the bed of greens. Split the walnuts and feta cheese between the two plates.

2. Drizzle each plate with 1½ teaspoons of olive oil and 1½ tablespoons of pickled beet brine. Season with salt and pepper. Serve.

PICKLE GRILLED CHEESE

MAKES 1 SANDWICH

Grilled cheese sandwiches are often served with pickles, but why not take the taste up a notch by adding the pickles to the actual sandwich? Pickles pair wonderfully with cheese, and even this basic sandwich can be taken to new heights with this simple addition. Use sourdough bread for its complementary tang or, if preferred, sub in a different variety.

PREP TIME: 10 minutes
COOK TIME: 6 minutes

2 slices sourdough bread

1½ teaspoons butter

1 ounce sharp cheddar cheese, thinly sliced

1 whole dill cucumber pickle (Quick Dill Pickles, page 36; Classic Dill Pickles, page 63; Spicy Dill Pickles, page 64; or Garlic Dill Pickles, page 65), thinly sliced

1. Heat a cast iron skillet over medium-high heat.

2. Butter one side of each slice of bread. Place the buttered side of one slice down in the skillet. Add the cheese and then the pickles. Top with the other slice of bread with the buttered side facing up.

3. Cook on the first side until golden brown and the cheese just starting to melt. Flip the sandwich and cook on the second side until browned and the cheese is melted. Serve.

TRY INSTEAD

Another interesting and quite delicious variation on this sandwich is a sauerkraut grilled cheese. Substitute a generous ½ cup of well-drained sauerkraut for the pickles and prepare the sandwich in the same way for a soured and savory sandwich with snap.

GRILLED FISH TACOS WITH PEACH AND MANGO SALSA

SERVES 4

Fish tacos are a great vehicle for enjoying the sweet, sour, and salty flavor of Peach and Mango Salsa (page 132). This ultra-fresh and light meal is a summertime favorite that can be savored with good company. While you're at it, prepare a Bloody Mary with Pickled Vegetables (page 147) to go along with it, and revel in all the outstanding flavors of the season.

PREP TIME: 15 minutes
COOK TIME: 30 minutes

1 tablespoon olive oil, plus more for the grill
1 teaspoon ground cumin
1 teaspoon ground coriander
1 teaspoon brown sugar
1½ pounds halibut, salmon, or other firm-fleshed fish
12 corn tortillas
1 recipe Peach and Mango Salsa (page 132)
1 avocado, sliced
1 lime, sliced (optional)

1. Prepare a grill to a medium-high heat. Oil the grates of the grill to prevent sticking.

2. In a small bowl, mix the cumin, coriander, and brown sugar.

3. Brush the fish with 1 tablespoon of olive oil and sprinkle with the spice mixture.

4. Grill the fish for 3 to 5 minutes per side, depending on the thickness of the fish. Flip once throughout cooking to enable a uniformly browned exterior. Remove the fish from the grill.

5. Place the tortillas on the grill to heat, flipping each once and cooking for about 10 to 20 seconds on each side.

6. Construct the tacos, splitting the fish between the tortillas. Top with a generous scoop of Peach and Mango Salsa and avocado slices. Squeeze with lime, if desired. Serve.

TRY INSTEAD

If barbecuing is not an option, heat a broiler to low and cook the fish under it for about 5 to 7 minutes on each side. This will create a similar texture to the fish without having to fire up the grill.

KIMCHI FRIED RICE

SERVES 2

Kimchi fried rice is quick to throw together and really pops in flavor. Use any variety of kimchi for this spicy side or light meal. Be sure to chop the kimchi into small pieces to allow the flavor to permeate all of the rice. If you prefer—and if it is not too spicy—add even more kimchi juice, and eliminate the salt altogether.

PREP TIME: 10 minutes
COOK TIME: 20 minutes

2 tablespoons canola oil

2 eggs

¾ cup finely chopped kimchi (Cabbage Kimchi, page 100; Cabbage, Carrot, Cucumber, and Broccoli Kimchi, page 101; Kale and Carrot Kimchi, page 102; Cucumber Kimchi, page 103)

2 cups cooked short-grain rice, preferably chilled

3 tablespoons kimchi juice

1 teaspoon salt

½ teaspoon freshly ground black pepper

1 scallion, thinly sliced

1. In a wok or large skillet, heat the canola oil over medium-high heat. Break the eggs into the pan and scramble them quickly before they set. Cook until just barely hard. Add the kimchi to the pan and mix well.

2. Mix in the rice and stir well to combine. Add the kimchi juice and continue mixing. Add the salt and the pepper. Divide the rice between two plates and garnish with the scallions.

A CLOSER LOOK

Due to its drier texture, day-old rice is best when making fried rice, so this is a perfect use of leftovers. Because the rice will be cold, it is important that you mix the rice and kimchi well and break up any clumps in the rice to prevent cold spots in the finished dish.

BANH MI SANDWICHES

SERVES 4

This Vietnamese sandwich may be quick to prepare, but that doesn't mean it skimps on flavor. Most of the ingredients for this can be found at a traditional grocery store. For the baguettes, you can either choose the light and airy variety used at a Vietnamese or Thai grocery, or use a traditional baguette, but stay away from those that are rustic or sourdough. For the best flavor, prepare this using leftover chicken or pork brought to room temperature.

PREP TIME: 15 minutes
COOK TIME: 5 minutes

4 (10-inch) baguettes

4 tablespoons mayonnaise

2 teaspoons Asian-style chili sauce

¾ pound leftover pork or chicken, sliced

1 recipe Vietnamese Pickled Daikon and Carrots (page 119)

½ cup cilantro leaves and stems

1. Heat the oven to 350°F.

2. Open the baguettes and place them on a baking sheet. Use your fingers to hollow out some of the baguettes, leaving a trough on both sides. Place them in the oven and toast them for about 5 minutes, until crisp on both sides. Remove from the oven and let them cool.

3. Spread one side of each baguette with 1 tablespoon of mayonnaise and a ½ teaspoon of the chili sauce. Split the meat between the sandwiches and top with a heaping ½ cup of pickled carrots and daikon. Add several sprigs of cilantro to each sandwich, close the baguettes, and cut each sandwich in half crosswise. Serve.

9

SUSHI ROLLS WITH TSUKEMONO

Sushi rolls need not be a treat enjoyed only in a Japanese restaurant. Once you prepare one or several types of tsukemono, it's easy to add them to these simple rolls and experience the sweet and salty combination of seasoned rice and seaweed with these umami-filled pickles. If you have seasoned sushi rice vinegar on hand, you can substitute that for the sugar, salt, and rice vinegar listed in the first step. You will need a bamboo rolling mat to form the sushi into rolls; if you don't have one, however, just make them into cones, or "hand rolls" as they are called.

PREP TIME: 30 minutes

3 cups cooked short-grain rice

⅓ cup rice vinegar

1 tablespoon sugar

1½ teaspoons salt

6 sheets of nori

1 recipe of Quick-Pickled Cucumbers (page 111), Sweet Pickled Cucumbers (page 112), Eggplant Pickled in Soy Sauce (page 110), or Bran Pickles (page 117)

½ pound imitation crab meat, shrimp tempura, or sushi-grade sashimi

Toasted sesame seeds

Soy sauce, for dipping

Wasabi paste, for dipping

1. Place the freshly cooked, hot rice in a large bowl. In a measuring cup, mix together the vinegar, sugar, and salt. Pour this over the rice, working quickly and flipping it together with the rice as you go. Avoid stirring, which breaks up the rice, and instead, flip the rice over several times until it has cooled.

2. Split each piece of nori in half lengthwise, using kitchen shears.

3. Cover the bamboo rolling mat with a layer of clear plastic wrap to prevent sticking. On the bamboo rolling mat, place one sheet of nori so that its longer side is parallel to the slats on the bamboo rolling mat. Add about ¼ cup of rice to the nori. Using wet hands to prevent sticking, spread the nori out to cover the sheet. Flip the nori over so that the rice is on the outside. Fill the roll with a couple strips of pickled vegetables along with your protein of choice. Be careful not to overfill it, as it will be difficult to close the roll.

4. Working from the bottom, roll the nori up tightly using the bamboo mat, applying pressure as you go. Sprinkle the roll with toasted sesame seeds. Repeat until all the rolls are filled.

5. Wet a clean kitchen towel, and rub it across the blade of a sharp knife. Cut each roll in half, and then slice each half into 1-inch rolls. Work quickly to prevent sticking, and if necessary, wet the blade with the kitchen towel again as you go.

A CLOSER LOOK

You can find fairly inexpensive bamboo rolling mats at most Asian grocery stores. You can also form the nori into cones, then stuff them with rice, pickled vegetables, and a protein of your choice.

COOKING WITH PICKLES

9

DIRTY DOZEN AND CLEAN FIFTEEN

A nonprofit and environmental watchdog organization called Environmental Working Group (EWG) looks at data supplied by the US Department of Agriculture (USDA) and the Food and Drug Administration (FDA) about pesticide residues and compiles a list each year of the best and worst pesticide loads found in commercial crops. You can refer to the Dirty Dozen list to know which fruits and vegetables you should always buy organic. The Clean Fifteen list lets you know which produce is considered safe enough when grown conventionally to allow you to skip the organics. This does not mean that the Clean Fifteen produce is pesticide-free, though, so wash these fruits and vegetables thoroughly.

These lists change every year, so make sure you look up the most recent before you fill your shopping cart. You'll find the most recent lists as well as a guide to pesticides in produce at EWG.org/FoodNews.

2015 DIRTY DOZEN

Apples	Peaches
Celery	Potatoes
Cherry tomatoes	Snap peas
Cucumbers	Spinach
Grapes	Strawberries
Nectarines	Sweet bell peppers

In addition to the Dirty Dozen, the EWG added two foods contaminated with highly toxic organo-phosphate insecticides:

Hot peppers	Kale/Collard greens

2015 CLEAN FIFTEEN

Asparagus	Mangos
Avocados	Onions
Cabbage	Papayas
Cantaloupe	Pineapples
Cauliflower	Sweet corn
Eggplant	Sweet peas (frozen)
Grapefruit	Sweet potatoes
Kiwis	

APPENDIX B

MEASUREMENT CONVERSIONS

VOLUME EQUIVALENTS (LIQUID)

US STANDARD	US STANDARD (OUNCES)	METRIC (APPROXIMATE)
2 tablespoons	1 fl. oz.	30 mL
¼ cup	2 fl. oz.	60 mL
½ cup	4 fl. oz.	120 mL
1 cup	8 fl. oz.	240 mL
1½ cups	12 fl. oz.	355 mL
2 cups or 1 pint	16 fl. oz.	475 mL
4 cups or 1 quart	32 fl. oz.	1 L
1 gallon	128 fl. oz.	4 L

VOLUME EQUIVALENTS (DRY)

US STANDARD	METRIC (APPROXIMATE)
⅛ teaspoon	0.5 mL
¼ teaspoon	1 mL
½ teaspoon	2 mL
¾ teaspoon	4 mL
1 teaspoon	5 mL
1 tablespoon	15 mL
¼ cup	59 mL
⅓ cup	79 mL
½ cup	118 mL
⅔ cup	156 mL
¾ cup	177 mL
1 cup	235 mL
2 cups or 1 pint	475 mL
3 cups	700 mL
4 cups or 1 quart	1 L

OVEN TEMPERATURES

FAHRENHEIT (F)	CELSIUS (C) (APPROXIMATE)
250°	120°
300°	150°
325°	165°
350°	180°
375°	190°
400°	200°
425°	220°
450°	230°

WEIGHT EQUIVALENTS

US STANDARD	METRIC (APPROXIMATE)
½ ounce	15 g
1 ounce	30 g
2 ounces	60 g
4 ounces	115 g
8 ounces	225 g
12 ounces	340 g
16 ounces or 1 pound	455 g

ALTITUDE ADJUSTMENTS

To make safe adjustments for canning at altitudes greater than 1,000 feet, use the following guidelines and consult resources such as the USDA's *Complete Guide to Home Canning* for more information. To find out your exact altitude, you can contact your local county extension agent or the local district conservationist for the Soil Conservation Service.

The technique for safe canning (see page 23) is the same, no matter what your altitude.

For **water-bath canning**, increase processing time as noted below based on your altitude.

ALTITUDE IN FEET	INCREASE PROCESSING TIME
0 to 1,000	no adjustment needed
1,001 to 3,000	5 minutes
3,001 to 6,000	10 minutes
6,001 to 8,000	15 minutes
8,001 to 10,000	20 minutes

For **pressure canning**, adjust pressure as noted below based on your altitude.

ALTITUDE IN FEET	DIAL GAUGE CANNER	WEIGHTED GAUGE CANNER
0 to 1,000	11	10
1,001 to 2,000	11	15
2,001 to 4,000	12	15
4,001 to 6,000	13	15
6,001 to 8,000	14	15
8,001 to 10,000	15	15

RESOURCES

SEEDS FOR GARDENING

Annie's Heirloom Seeds:
www.anniesheirloomseeds.com

Uprising Seeds: www.uprisingorganics.com

SPICES

Mountain Rose Herbs:
www.mountainroseherbs.com

Penzeys Spices: www.penzeys.com

CANNING AND FERMENTATION SUPPLIES

Ball: www.freshpreserving.com/products

Cultures for Health: www.culturesforhealth.com
/natural-fermentation/fermentation-crocks.html

Pickl-It: www.pickl-it.com

REFERENCES

Abbas, Abul K., Andrew H. Lichtman, and Shiv Pillai. *Basic Immunology: Functions and Disorders of the Immune System*. 4th ed. Philadelphia: Saunders, 2012.

American Autoimmune. "Autoimmune Statistics." Accessed June 15, 2014. www.aarda.org/autoimmune-information/autoimmune-statistics.

Gardeners and Farmers of Terre Vivante. *Keeping Food Fresh*. White River Junction, Vermont: Chelsea Green Publishing Company, 1999.

Hisamatsu, Ikuko. *Tsukemono: Japanese Pickling Recipes*. Tokyo: Japan Publications Trading Co. Ltd, 2005.

Karlin, Mary. *Mastering Fermentation*. New York: Ten Speed Press, 2013.

Krissoff, Liana. *Canning for a New Generation*. New York: Stewart, Tabori & Chang, 2010.

McClelland, Marisa. *Food in Jars*. Philadelphia: Running Press, 2011.

Rockridge Press. *DIY Canning: Over 100 Small-Batch Recipes for All Seasons*. Berkeley, Rockridge Press, 2015.

Williams, David. "Digestive Health Benefits of Traditional Fermented Food." Dr. David Williams. Accessed May 15, 2015. www.drdavidwilliams.com/traditional-fermented-foods-benefits.

Wood, Rebecca. *The New Whole Foods Encyclopedia*. New York: Penguin Books, 2010.

INDEX

ALSO IN THE DIY SERIES

Steep-by-steep (and step-by-step) recipes to create your own fresh, fragrant, and fizzy kombucha.

AVAILABLE NOW
$12.99 paperback / $6.99 ebook

Enjoy homemade sauerkraut, kimchi, kombucha, kefir, yogurt, and other probiotic delights.

AVAILABLE NOW
$12.99 paperback / $6.99 ebook

Preserve nature's bounty and enjoy seasonal ingredients throughout the year.

AVAILABLE NOW
$12.99 paperback / $6.99 ebook

Achieve homebrew mastery with these tried and tested craft beer recipes.

AVAILABLE NOW
$12.99 paperback / $6.99 ebook

9 781623 156633